EXPLORATION OF AFRICA

There are six new HORIZON CARAVEL BOOKS published each year. The titles now available are:

EXPLORATION OF AFRICA
NELSON AND THE AGE OF FIGHTING SAIL
ALEXANDER THE GREAT
RUSSIA UNDER THE CZARS
HEROES OF POLAR EXPLORATION
KNIGHTS OF THE CRUSADES

American Heritage also publishes AMERICAN HERITAGE JUNIOR LIBRARY books, a similar series on American history. The titles now available are:

LEXINGTON, CONCORD AND BUNKER HILL
CLIPPER SHIPS AND CAPTAINS
D-DAY, THE INVASION OF EUROPE
WESTWARD ON THE OREGON TRAIL
THE FRENCH AND INDIAN WARS
GREAT DAYS OF THE CIRCUS
STEAMBOATS ON THE MISSISSIPPI
COWBOYS AND CATTLE COUNTRY
TEXAS AND THE WAR WITH MEXICO
THE PILGRIMS AND PLYMOUTH COLONY
THE CALIFORNIA GOLD RUSH
PIRATES OF THE SPANISH MAIN
TRAPPERS AND MOUNTAIN MEN
MEN OF SCIENCE AND INVENTION
NAVAL BATTLES AND HEROES
THOMAS JEFFERSON AND HIS WORLD
DISCOVERERS OF THE NEW WORLD
RAILROADS IN THE DAYS OF STEAM
INDIANS OF THE PLAINS
THE STORY OF YANKEE WHALING

COVER: *Trumpeting defiantly, an African elephant is fired on by explorers on the Zambezi.*
ROYAL GEOGRAPHICAL SOCIETY

FRONT ENDSHEET: *A French artist noted how an expedition crossed this African river.*
Journal of a Residence in Ashanti, DUPUIS, 1824

BACK ENDSHEET: *Ashanti tribesmen demonstrate their loyalty to a British ambassador.*
Journal of a Residence in Ashanti, DUPUIS, 1824

TITLE PAGE: *Explorer Dixon Denham was sketched standing on the shores of Lake Chad.*
Tales of Travels in Central Africa, SNELLING, 1831

A HORIZON CARAVEL BOOK

EXPLORATION OF AFRICA

By the Editors of
HORIZON MAGAZINE

Author
THOMAS STERLING

Consultant
GEORGE H. T. KIMBLE
Professor of Geography, Indiana University

ILLUSTRATED WITH PAINTINGS, DRAWINGS, AND MAPS OF THE PERIOD

Published by American Heritage Publishing Co., Inc.
Book trade distribution by Meredith Press
Institutional distribution by Harper & Row, Publishers

FIRST EDITION
Library of Congress Catalogue Card Number: 63-11738

NATIONAL ARCHIVES OF RHODESIA AND NYASALAND

As he was not an artist, Livingstone engaged Thomas Baines to paint the pictorial record of his 1858 Zambezi expedition. One of Baines' watercolors (above) shows another member of the party in pursuit of an elephant.

FOREWORD

Journal of the Discovery of the Sources of the Nile, SPEKE, 1864

Two cultures meet: a British explorer dances with an African queen.

When the explorer René Caillié returned to France from Africa in 1828, he published a sketch of the legendary city he had discovered—Timbuctoo. But neither that simple drawing nor his matter-of-fact description gave Caillié's countrymen a sufficiently colorful picture to match their preconceptions of how Africa should look. They turned their backs on the young explorer, ignored his accomplishments, and let him die neglected.

Medieval map makers had found a way to make up for their geographical ignorance: they cluttered the emptiness of Africa with brightly illuminated cities and fantastic creatures. That graphic tradition was broken when, instead of works of dramatic power and artistic splendor, explorers like Caillié brought back unsophisticated sketches in which the facts of the continent spoke for themselves. The men who opened up Africa in the nineteenth century were more interested in discovery, in the ways and means of exploration, and in survival than in glorification. Their drawings have an immediacy that brings the explorers to life even today, more than one hundred years later.

This book is filled with such firsthand impressions. It also contains selections from the great wealth of native art that now exists in museums within and outside Africa. And to show regions of which neither explorers nor natives made a contemporaneous record, modern photographs have been used.

A few serious artists finally did travel to Africa—like Thomas Baines, who went with Livingstone and painted the elephant hunt on the opposite page. Their rarely seen works, and the more informal body of African explorer art, deserve to be recognized now as a vibrant part of Africa's—and the world's—heritage.

THE EDITORS

David Livingstone used this station at Kongone, on the Zambezi delta, as a base camp for exploring inland along the river Shire and into Lake Nyasa.

CONTENTS

I

Picturesque Views of the River Niger, ALLEN, 1840

MUNGO PARK: EXPLORER

The great river was silver-gray and sluggish in the mid-morning heat. Its banks were low, and on the opposite shore a large town could be seen. The buildings were square and made of clay, with flat roofs; some were two stories high and many were whitewashed. From a distance they stood out like a mirage, receding and approaching in the glaring light. Graceful minarets soared above the narrow streets. That was how the African town of Ségou appeared one July morning in 1796. A young man named Mungo Park sat in the sand by the river, watching the huge canoes which had been carved from logs carrying hundreds of people, and even horses, across the current to the market. He was twenty-five years old, alone, without funds, and starving. But in his diary he noted that he took "infinite pleasure" in the scene. More important, he noted which way the river was flowing: east.

The river that the young Scotsman was gazing at was the Niger, which had been a cause of wonder and speculation for centuries. The classical Greek historian and geographer Herodotus had reported a great river flowing eastward in this western part of Africa. But more recent geographers held contrary opinions; they assumed that the river must flow west and have some connection with the Nile.

It was Park's assignment to do away with these rumors and assumptions by means of discovery. Fourteen months previous, in May of 1795, this former ship's surgeon had appeared at the London offices of the recently founded African Association to volunteer his services. He was simply seeking adventure. But the objectives of the backers of the African Association were more serious; they wanted Africa to be explored thoroughly so that trade could be initiated, and they believed that the Niger River was the place to begin. So far the attempts had been costly and unsuccessful—three explorers had died of illness or been

Flying the British flag, a two-boat expedition went down the Niger in 1830. Natives swarmed to meet it (left), and one of their long canoes capsized.

murdered by natives before they could report anything about the strategic river. Park was accepted as the next man to try.

He had little idea of the peoples or of the country he would have to pass through to accomplish his mission. When he arrived on the west coast of Africa it was the rainy season; almost immediately he caught one of the violent fevers that have always plagued African explorers. But he bore it and survived, using the six months' delay to learn the native language.

The Life and Travels of Mungo Park, PARK, 1799

This drawing of Park's encounter with a lion appears on the title page of his book. He and his guide were terrified; but he wrote, "It is probable the lion was not hungry, for he quietly suffered us to pass."

The remarkable journey that he took from there to the banks of the Niger began on December 2, 1795. He pushed into the interior from the mouth of the Gambia River (see map on page 20) with two servants, one horse, and two donkeys. Six other travelers accompanied him, two of whom were slave traders, members of Africa's richest and vilest profession.

Park had been instructed by his employers in the African Association to carry very little with him; other travelers in Africa had been killed for their possessions. In addition to the small assortment of beads, amber, and tobacco that he carried for gifts and for trading purposes, he had provisions for only two days and but little money. Among his other scant possessions were a pocket sextant, a compass, a thermometer, two rifles, two pairs of pistols, and an umbrella. He was eventually to be stripped of everything but his horse and his compass.

The first stage of the journey was relatively easy. Park's little expedition went safely among the Negro tribes who lived between the Atlantic coast and the Niger River just below the Sahara desert. The countryside was thickly wooded brushland, rising gently here and there to ledges of red ironstone and falling back to fertile valleys. Aside from the heat, there was nothing outwardly savage about the landscape. There were wild animals, of course, but the chief danger lay simply in being at the mercy of the tribesmen—many of whom had recently been converted to Mohammedanism. Religious or not, they were totally indifferent to the travelers' hunger and thirst.

Then one day, when the expedition had been on the move for nearly a month, it was waylaid by the warriors of a tribal chieftain. They robbed Park of half of his scant goods, claiming that he had tried to slip away without paying the fee that was due their chief.

Both servants urged the young Scotsman to turn back. They were being sensible, not cowardly; they saw that Park,

NATIONAL PORTRAIT GALLERY, LONDON

Mungo Park, lured by curiosity to the heart of Africa, is seen in this miniature. It was made from a painting by Henry Edridge—the only portrait ever done of Park.

whose money was running out, did not have the resources, the experience, or the natural ability to break through the obstacles of African travel. The little party began to live with the constant threat of starvation. And when they finally came into more friendly territory, the local ruler merely entertained them until he had a well-calculated idea of how much he could take. Having demanded and been given most of Park's remaining goods, the ruler sent him on his way.

Also, the threat of war was in the air. The village drums beat martial tempos; horns were blown as bands of horse-mounted warriors assembled; and the normal, delicately balanced system of bribery and terror that united the tribes was giving way. Park was told on February 12, when he arrived in the territory of Kaarta, that he was just in time for the outbreak of hostilities.

The throne of the king of Kaarta was crude—a mound of earth with a leopard skin flung over it—but his words were kindly. He too suggested that Park go back. If the king survived the war, which he estimated would take from three to four months, he would be glad to receive the explorer as a guest again and send him on toward the great river. In any case, he warned that if Park tried to cross from Kaarta into the territory of the enemy he would surely be taken for a spy and killed. The only possible route, if he insisted on proceeding, was north around the battle zone and then back to the Niger at Ségou—though this was also dangerous. Why go on?

The next day Park sent the king his pistols and his holsters as a gift and then headed northeast into the dry bushland bordering the Sahara. Now only one servant accompanied him—the other had started back to the Gambia with the explorer's papers, and the rest of the party had separated. Park and his servant circled for days, suffering from thirst and harassed by the nomadic Moslems, whom Park referred to as Moors. Then, as he was about to enter Ségou and was almost within sight of the Niger, Park was taken prisoner by the troops of Ali, the Moslem king of Ludamar.

In his writings, Park reserved his greatest hatred for these near-white Moslems of the southwestern Sahara. Although he passed among many of their tribes safely, he never felt secure. By contrast, he felt much at home in Negro—or "black"—Africa, where he found the people more civilized, unused to wanton cruelty, and frequently generous and kind.

Five days after he was captured, Park was brought into Chief Ali's nomadic encampment. The land here in the north was intensely dry and covered with stunted acacia shrub. It was almost impossible to travel after noon. There was a hot, dry wind, as there is now, which will split a man's lips in a few hours and dry his eyes until they feel brittle and ready to crack.

In the following days Park was tormented in a thousand petty ways. When he fell sick with fever his captors deliberately teased him and tried to make him feel worse. All of his belongings were taken except his compass, which he had buried in the sandy floor of his hut. But during all this time he preserved a stoic calm and tried to make himself as inconspicuous as possible. That, he learned, was the secret of survival. It was not courage in the sense that that quality is usually known; it was nothing more than the willingness to be humiliated. But he wondered whether the death that had come to earlier explorers might not be better.

Moving inland from the West African coast, Park's party crossed the upper Senegal on a floating bridge made of bamboo. The man seated in the lower right corner of this picture is believed to be Park himself.

At last, when Park had almost given up any hope of being released, he was allowed to accompany Chief Ali to a southern part of the territory where he believed it would be easier to make good an escape. And Park did escape from Ali, with the few belongings which had been returned to him: two shirts, two pairs of trousers, two pocket handkerchiefs, an upper and an under waistcoat, a hat, a pair of halfboots, and a cloak. He counted the items carefully,

This carving of a sour-faced woman was made by the Ibibio natives of Nigeria, through whose territory Park passed. When in use, as part of a male dancer's headdress, the figure's arms swing threateningly.

knowing they might save his life, and tied them in a bundle. Then at daybreak on July 2, he cautiously slipped out of Ali's camp and set out on his ill-fed horse for Ségou. Almost immediately he was waylaid on the road by a new band of tribesmen who eventually decided that stealing his cloak was better than killing him or returning him to Ali.

He proceeded through a wooded country, looking vainly for water and food, and at last was so weakened by thirst that he fell to the sand and could not rise. "Here then," he thought ". . . terminate all my hopes of being useful in my day and generation; here must the short span of my life come to an end." Toward evening, however, a light rain refreshed him and he determined to begin again. For almost another month he stumbled on—always toward the Niger—begging what he could and occasionally buying grain for his pitiful horse with bits of clothing and odd buttons until he came to his goal.

When he finally reached the river and glimpsed the houses and mosques of Ségou across the slowly flowing water, he sat down exhausted in the sand. He knew that now he could only wait until the ruler of Ségou decided whether to block his passage or let him proceed. Without an invitation, he dared not even make the short boat trip across the river to the king's palace.

At the end of the day a representative from the king came over to Park. He pointed to a distant village and told the Scotsman to stay there and await further orders. There was little indication that the orders would ever come. After risking his health, his freedom, and his life to accomplish what few other men could, or would, have done, Park now saw that he must turn back within sight of his goal.

He did stay in the region for two more weeks, making one short trip down the Niger; but his heart was no longer in the adventure. Although the ruler of Ségou, whom he never saw, eventually sent him five thousand cowries—small shells that were used as money throughout West Africa—he did not have enough funds, or strength, to go on. At last he began the long journey back to the coast.

Park arrived in England almost a year and a half later. There he was astonished to find that he was not considered a failure. The book that he wrote of his travels was eagerly received; his courage was hailed; he was regarded as an explorer.

Park's return coincided with an upsurge of British interest in Africa and things African. Both the merchants, who wanted new markets, and the scholars, who wanted to

TEXT CONTINUED ON PAGE 22

THE MUSEUM OF PRIMITIVE ART, NEW YORK

The most sophisticated kingdom in the Niger area was Benin, one of whose craftsmen carved a warrior and two fish on this bronze plaque.

ALL: *L'Afrique*, LYONS, 1821

BIBLIOTHEQUE NATIONALE

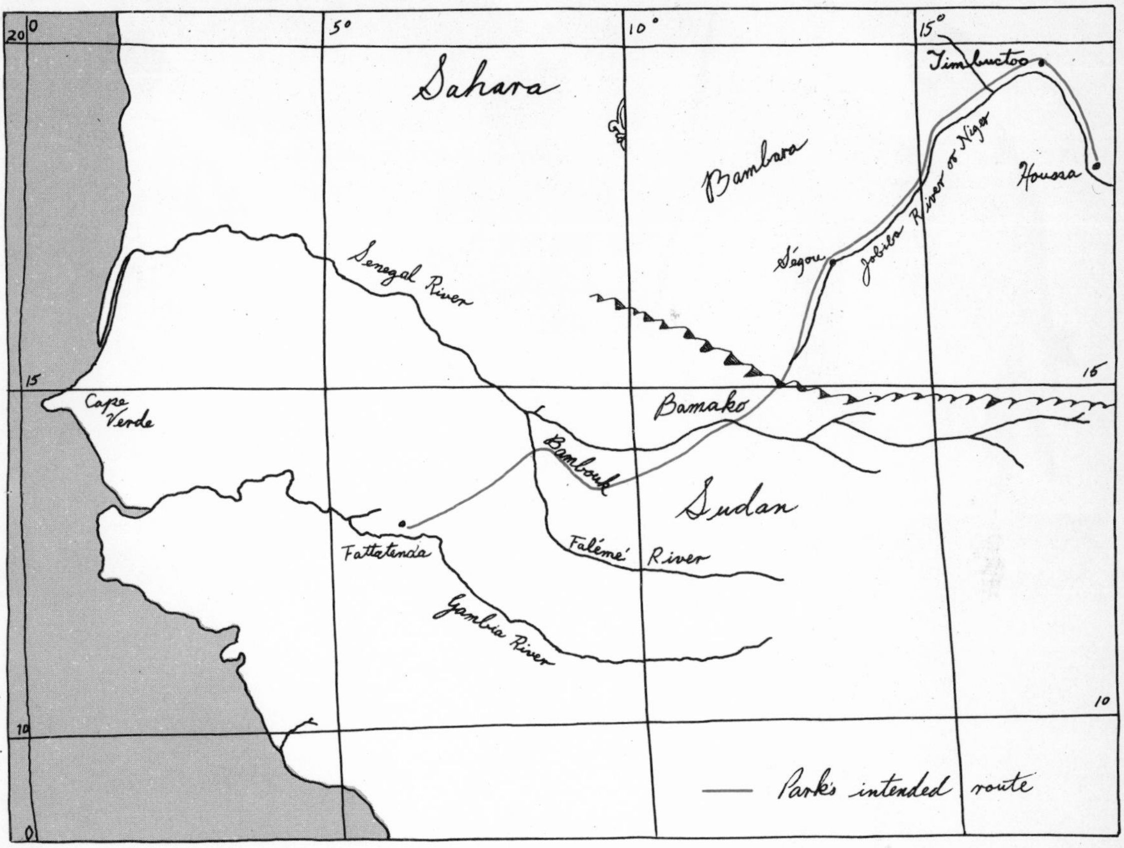

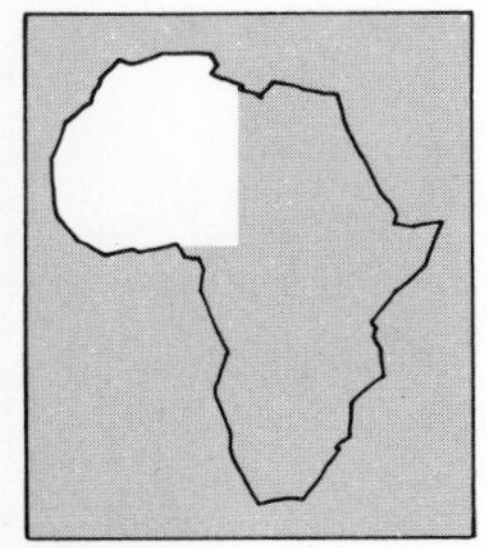

PARK'S WEST AFRICA

In the fourteenth-century map at far left, a richly garbed Negro king sits on his throne, awaiting the approach of a mounted Moslem merchant. Both are West Africans, but they are men of two different worlds: the Moslem is from the Sahara, which stretches north to the Atlas Mountains; the Negro is from the Sudan, a belt of desert, semi-arid grassland, and bush that extends across the continent between the Sahara and the Guinea coast. By 1795, when Mungo Park arrived in West Africa (shown as white section on Africa map at left), the Sudanese kingdoms had declined; but Moslems who came south across the Sahara ("Ashara" on the map) still traded there. And the veiled Tuaregs, three of whom are shown at left above, preyed on the camel caravans. Park's intended route through the Sudan is shown on the map above, reconstructed from the explorer's original sketch; but after encountering warring tribesmen near Bambouk, he had to make a detour into the Sahara territories.

OVERLEAF: *By the end of the nineteenth century, the face of Africa had been crisscrossed by tracks of explorers. Arrows here indicate the direction of their routes.*

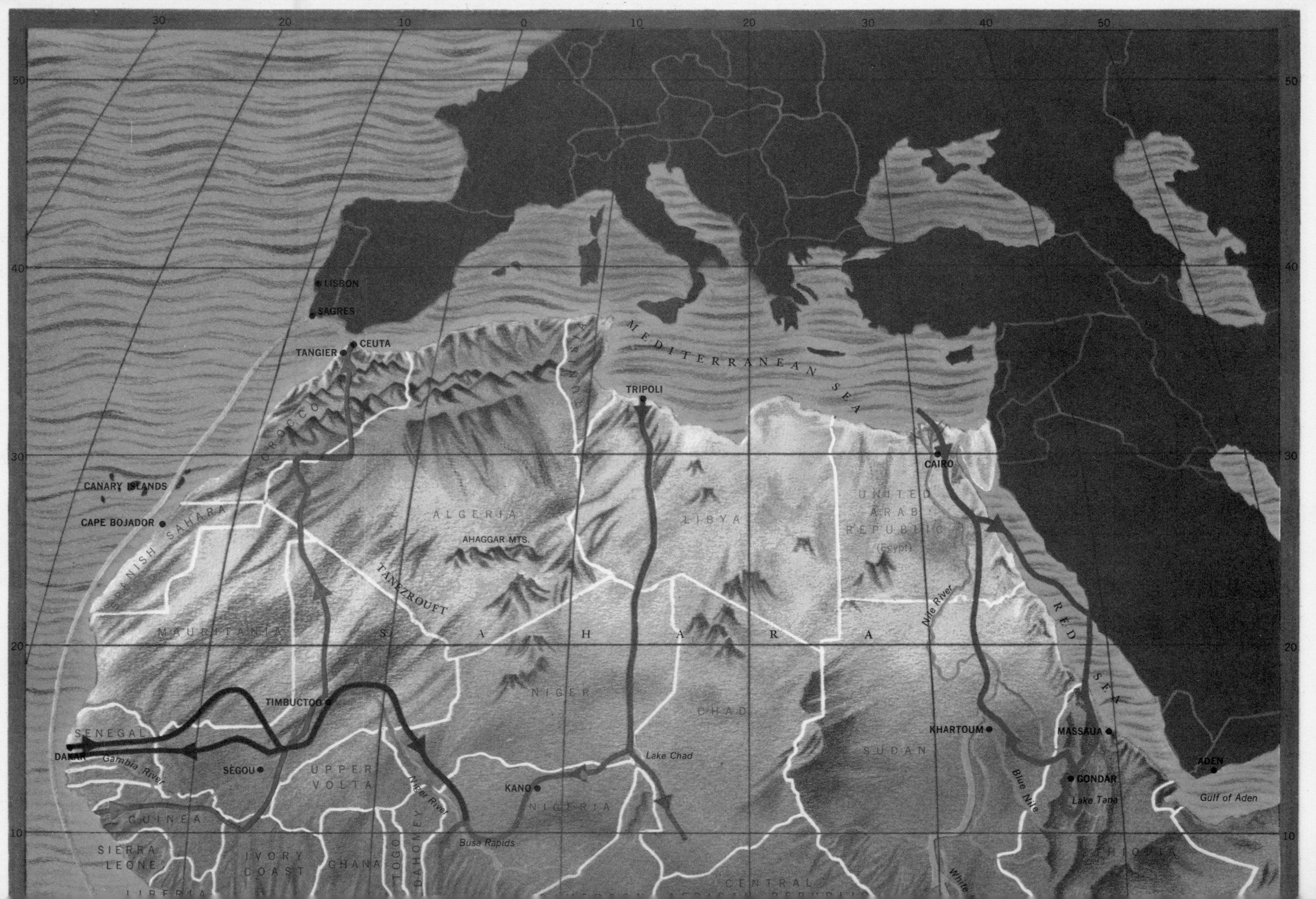
LISBON
SAGRES
TANGIER
CEUTA
MEDITERRANEAN SEA
TRIPOLI
CAIRO
CANARY ISLANDS
CAPE BOJADOR
SPANISH SAHARA
MOROCCO
ALGERIA
AHAGGAR MTS.
TANEZROUFT
LIBYA
UNITED ARAB REPUBLIC
(Egypt)
Nile River
RED SEA
SAHARA
MAURITANIA
NIGER
CHAD
SUDAN
TIMBUCTOO
KHARTOUM
MASSAUA
ADEN
SENEGAL
DAKAR
Gambia River
SEGOU
UPPER VOLTA
Niger River
KANO
NIGERIA
Lake Chad
Blue Nile
GONDAR
Lake Tana
Gulf of Aden
GUINEA
SIERRA LEONE
IVORY COAST
GHANA
TOGO
DAHOMEY
Busa Rapids
CENTRAL
White

AFRICAN EXPLORATION
Routes of Explorers
da Gama: 1497-98
Bruce: 1768-73
Park: 1795-1805
Denham, Clapperton, Lander: 1822-34
Caillié: 1827-28
Speke with Burton, Grant: 1856-63
Livingstone: 1841-73
Stanley: 1871-89
SCALE OF MILES
0
250
500
AFRICA'S POSITION ON THE WORLD MAP
Gulf of Guinea
ATLANTIC OCEAN
INDIAN OCEAN
EQUATOR
EQUATOR
RÍO MUNI
GABON
THE CONGO
(Brazzaville)
Congo River
MATADI
THE CONGO
(Leopoldville)
LUANDA
ANGOLA
SOUTH WEST AFRICA
Stanley Falls
STANLEYVILLE
Aruwimi River
Lake Albert
Murchison Falls
RUWENZORI MTS.
(Mts. of the Moon)
UGANDA
KENYA
SOMALI
Lake Edward
RUANDA
Lake Kivu
URUNDI
Lake Victoria
Luama River
Lualaba River
UJIJI
TABORA
MOMBASA
ZANZIBAR
BAGAMOYO
Lake Tanganyika
TANGANYIKA
Lake Mweru
NYASALAND
Lake Nyasa
Ruvuma River
COMORO ISLANDS
NORTHERN RHODESIA
SOUTHERN RHODESIA
Zambezi River
TETE
Shire River
SESHEKE
LIVINGSTONE
Victoria Falls
MOZAMBIQUE
MADAGASCAR
Lake Ngami
BECHUANALAND
KALAHARI DESERT
Orange River
SOUTH AFRICA
St. Helena Bay
CAPE TOWN
Mossel Bay

TEXT CONTINUED FROM PAGE 17
complete their picture of the world, were eager to push expeditions forward into the continent. News of Park's partially successful trip spread, and attention was focused even more keenly on the eastward-flowing Niger River: it seemed to be the key to Africa's mysterious heart.

So Park, his faith in himself restored, was sent back to continue his quest. He led a government-sponsored expedition that was very different from his first lonely effort. He was given ample funds and was empowered to enlist soldiers from the British West African base of Gambia.

But things went badly from the beginning. Because of delays in England, the fifty-six-man party had to set out as the rainy season was about to begin. Before they reached the Niger on August 19, 1805, all but eleven members of the expedition were dead of fever. Park and the remaining men struggled to build a small boat, and they finally succeeded in launching it. They called their frail craft His Majesty's Schooner *Joliba*, after the river's native name.

As they floated down the river, each new turning brought a new discovery, a new peril. Because the river continued to flow east, but somewhat north, some of the party thought that it *was* the Nile, as the geographers had foretold. Park himself assumed that the river would soon turn south and they would see it was the Congo.

What happened to them in that autumn of 1805 is still not entirely known. Park's diary, which was brought back by one of his servants, indicated that they drifted north to Timbuctoo, then south with the river into the country now named Nigeria. The natives who lived along the river became increasingly hostile, coming out after the explorers in larger and more tumultuous war parties. Then, according to a guide who was put ashore just before Park and his companions disappeared, they were attacked by the river dwellers at a place where the Niger's banks come close together. When the *Joliba* was about to be overwhelmed, Park and a young lieutenant leaped into the water, taking with them the other two Europeans who were ill. This was the last that was seen of them.

Park's hope was to get the men to safety, even at the risk of his own life. In that final act of courage he failed, and he failed to navigate the Niger to its mouth. But in the judgment of his contemporaries, Park had proved himself an explorer; his scouting of the river was an important first link in the chain of discovery that Europeans were to stretch across Africa in the nineteenth century.

Before the climax of his second expedition, Park passed Kabara, shown at right with the Niger in the background. This town is Timbuctoo's port on the river. Park had reinforced his party with men from an English fort (below) on the Gambia.

PHOTO BY ERNEST DUNBAR

Drafts of Guinea, SMITH, 1732

ARMADA DE NVNO DA CVNHA

inha q̃ se pasou a esta naueta

nuno da cu nha q̃ se per deo na Ilha de São Lço

d.te da sequa

Fco de mendonça

bernaldim da silua no par cel de sofala

Afonso vaz azanbuio na ylha de joam da noua

II

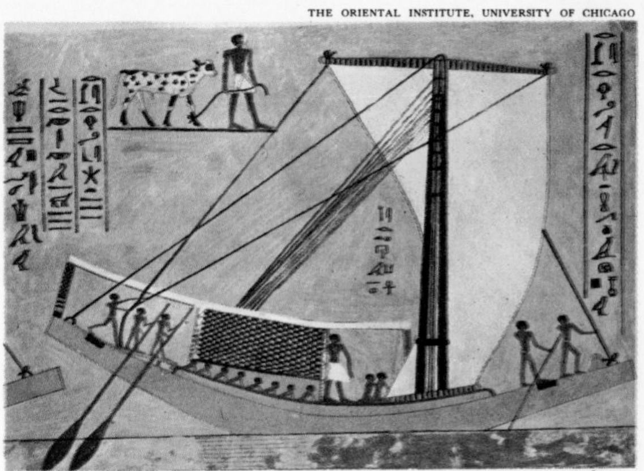

CARAVELS OF PORTUGAL

Nearly four centuries before Mungo Park set off for the Niger, two inquisitive Portuguese diplomats visited the North African city of Ceuta. The year was 1413, and the story they gave out was that they were bound for Sicily to arrange a marriage between the Sicilian queen and the second son of their master, the king of Portugal. The inhabitants of Ceuta, the Moors, whose language was Arabic but whose racial lineage was uncertain, let the visitors roam about the city in peace. Eventually the Portuguese ship sailed off again into the Mediterranean.

The Moors would have done well to ask themselves why the queen of Sicily would consider marrying a prince who was not the direct heir to the throne of Portugal. She would not; the diplomatic journey was a hoax. The real purpose of the visitors was to make a report on the defenses of the city to their king, John I, who was considering launching an invasion from Portugal across into Africa.

The two Portuguese spies were African explorers of a sort, though their adventure was totally unlike that of Mungo Park on the Niger River. Indeed, there were many journeys to and through Africa long before the geography of the continent captured the imagination of nineteenth-

The Egyptians sailed along the coasts of Africa 3,500 years ago—in ships like the one in the tomb painting above. Better suited for exploration were Portuguese caravels, seen at left in a sixteenth-century watercolor.

Necho II of Egypt (right) is said to have sent the first expedition around Africa, but the geographer Ptolemy denied this could be done. He drew a map (above) in which the southern portion of Africa was linked to Asia. Much later, under the command of Henry the Navigator (far right), Portuguese seamen proved that the continent of Africa could be circumnavigated.

century Europe. But many of these early voyages were undertaken in secret; they were far removed from each other in time and in country of origin, and few of the maps resulting from them were of much help to later explorers.

On most medieval maps of Africa, the Mediterranean shore was plotted fairly accurately, but beyond that the coast was shown as a vague and wandering line between a few known points, and the interior of the continent was filled with pictures of mythical kings and fantastic creatures.

Long before Christ, the ancient Egyptians built a nation that had the strength and imagination to expand beyond the confines of the Nile Valley. An Egyptian mariner who left a record of his voyage on a stone tablet—which would be more helpful if it contained his name and the date of the voyage—sailed down the Red Sea to the coast of what is now Somalia. And there exists a subsequent report of an expedition organized by Pharaoh Necho II and manned by Phoenician sailors that supposedly circumnavigated the continent about 600 B.C. But the Egyptians, for all their love of their own land and its ever-flowing river, had no enduring interest in the extent or the shape of Africa, and men soon forgot the little that had been discovered.

The outline of the African continent would not become known until a race of seamen appeared who had the boldness and the technical ability to follow the route of the

UNIVERSITY MUSEUM, UNIVERSITY OF PENNSYLVANIA

BIBLIOTHEQUE NATIONALE

ancient pharaoh's legendary expedition around Africa.

These sailor-explorers were the fifteenth-century Portuguese, and their leader was Prince Henry, who first took an interest in Africa when he and his brother devised the plan of winning their knighthood by attacking Ceuta. The princes' first problem was to persuade their father that the attack could succeed.

The reports the two spies had brought back to King John differed completely, yet the king found both of them encouraging. At first he had been skeptical, suspecting that his sons' plan to attack the Moorish city was but youthful foolhardiness. For the Moors were reputed to be able fighters, and almost nothing was known of their country. A century and a half before, Christians had tried to capture the North African city of Tunis from its Moslem rulers in an ill-fated campaign that came to be called the Eighth Crusade. But King John was as ambitious as his sons, and he was willing to listen to the men who had seen Ceuta with their own eyes.

In this detail from a map, Prester John appears as an Ethiopian king.

The first of them, Captain Alfonso Furtado, said that military considerations were unimportant—as were his own impressions of the fortifications. Much more important, he believed, was the fact that years before on the African coast he had met an old man who told him that a king of Spain or Portugal would be the first monarch to win possessions in Africa. It was clear to Captain Furtado, in a mystical way that made sense to men of the Middle Ages, that this new crusade had been preordained by God.

Heartened but unconvinced, the king then turned to the second voyager, a knightly prior of the Hospitaller order. The prior called for "two sacks of sand, a roll of ribbon, a half-bushel of beans, and a basin." Before the king's astonished eyes he proceeded to make a three-dimensional model of Ceuta. And it was obvious from the model that the city could be taken.

King John immediately ordered that a survey of his galleys and flatboats be made. But he also ordered that plans for the invasion proceed with the utmost secrecy. If word of them reached the Moors, they would mobilize the vast numbers of men at their command—tribesmen from the unknown southern reaches of the continent—and Ceuta would be made impregnable. The secret was kept.

When the Portuguese fleet arrived in the Strait of Gibraltar and came within sight of Ceuta, the Moors were taken completely by surprise. But they were spared the terror of a lightning assault, for the wind blew most of the

Portuguese fleet right past the city and into the Mediterranean. There was time to close the gates of the city, and the inhabitants climbed upon the walls to get a better view of the enemy. What they saw—the ships being swept down the coast—made them think they had been saved, and they dismissed the troops that had been hastily called up from the interior when the Portuguese first appeared.

Four days later, the Moors paid for their overconfidence. For the invasion fleet returned and drew up along the shore. A Portuguese squire who could not bear to wait any longer jumped into a landing craft and ordered the rowers to take him in. Prince Henry followed, commanding the trumpeters to sound the attack. Five hundred Portuguese stormed onto the beach, and after a fierce struggle pushed the Moors back to the gates of the city. Prince Henry, who had led the attack, held up his men until rein-

Prince Henry founded his scientific academy at Sagres on the southwest tip of Europe. The building was destroyed long ago; today another fort stands in ruins on its site.

PHOTO BY YAN

forcements could arrive from the ships. He and his brother agreed that the combined force should then be split up: Henry would press forward with the frontal assault on the city, and his brother would seize the heights commanding Ceuta on the landward side.

Prince Henry then charged once more at the city, and his rush carried him through a gate into the main street. There the tightly packed men hacked away at the Moors with their halberds and swords but could not drive them farther back. At one point, having gained the upper hand,

The port of Ceuta (formerly Septa) was Henry's first African conquest. This picture of the famous walled city is from a 1594 French atlas.

THE BOIES PENROSE LIBRARY

Historia da Expansao Portuguesa no Mundo

Portugal sent soldiers to Africa after Ceuta was won. They were armed like troops in the sixteenth-century Portuguese tapestry above.

the Moors threatened to rout the Portuguese, and Henry found himself almost alone in a sea of Moors. The chronicler Zurara described the moment vividly. He wrote that Henry, who "was then but twenty-one years of age and whose limbs were vigorous and his courage very great . . . was overcome with rage, and running on the Moors assailed them so strongly that . . . he scattered them."

The Moors retreated to the citadel, the city's stronghold. When Prince Henry reached its gate, he had only seventeen knights and attendants left. Of these, four survived the furious fighting that continued for the next two and a half hours. Henry was finally persuaded to give up the battle and join his brother, who had succeeded in taking the city's mosque. There they spent the night, planning the next day's attack. But when a guard detachment reported that there was no sound from the citadel—a flock of sparrows were resting there quietly, undisturbed by any inhabitants—the two men knew there was no need to fight further. Ceuta belonged to Portugal; it was the first foothold to be gained in Africa by Europeans since the days of Roman conquest.

Prince Henry earned his knighthood as a result of the successful invasion. It was also in Ceuta that he became forever smitten with a fascination for Africa. His imagination was fired by what he saw in the bazaars and storehouses—wares from the East brought overland across the desert. And undoubtedly it was in Ceuta that Henry heard of the Christian kingdom on the other side of the desert, the domain of the legendary Prester John.

That ruler, who was reported to reside either in the jungles of Africa or in the deserts of Asia, was alleged to be boundlessly rich and powerful. Inspired by these tales, Prince Henry, the newly appointed governor of Ceuta, developed a master plan: he would explore the coasts of Africa until he found a way to the land of Prester John; then their combined forces would outflank the Moslem countries on the Mediterranean and win total victory over the infidel. This scheme of discovery and conquest seemed more important to Henry than any of his other duties. In 1419 he left the royal palace and retired to a lonely promontory called Sagres, on the southern tip of Portugal. There, in his little fortress, he studied and planned; in the process, he created the world's first academy of navigation.

The seafarers sent out from Portugal as a result of Prince Henry's plan sailed in new vessels called caravels, which represented a great improvement over the old fishing smacks, or *barcas*, in which the Portuguese had already voyaged far into the Atlantic. The *barcas* had one stubby mast on which was hung a square sail that allowed them to go only before the wind. But the graceful caravels that Henry's shipbuilders were now constructing had two or three masts with newly designed sails and rigging that allowed them to maneuver far more freely. And the men themselves were as vital to Henry's scheme as were ships and improved navigation instruments. Experienced, adventuresome, and eager to carry their cross and their flag to the ends of the earth, the Portuguese mariners responded brilliantly to their prince's challenge.

In 1418 the Madeira island group was sighted, and in 1432 the Azores were found by Gonçalo Velho Cabral. Two years later, fearsome Cape Bojador was rounded by Gil Eanes, Prince Henry's squire. The squire came back to Sagres with the reassuring news that the coastline and the sea beyond Cape Bojador were no more formidable than the waters they had always known. But before Prince Henry died in 1460, reports were brought back that the coast of

TEXT CONTINUED ON PAGE 38

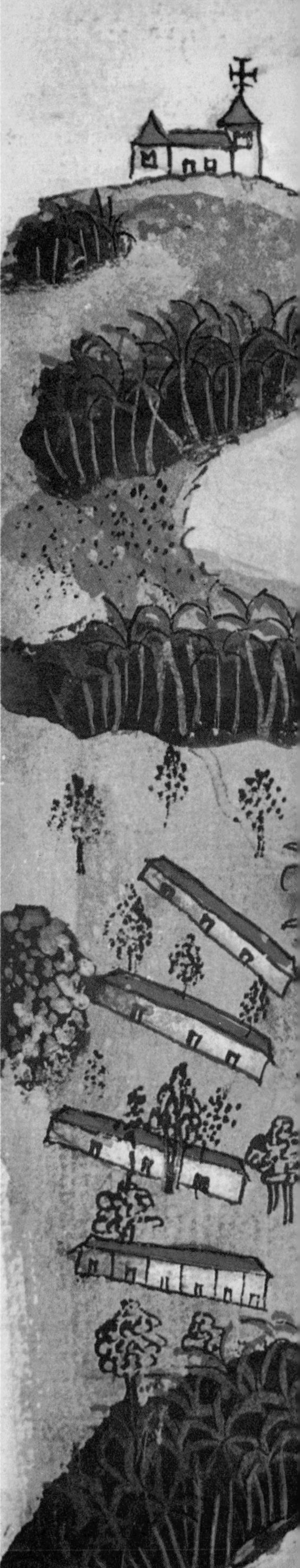

In this handsome watercolor from a rare manuscript on navigation, Portuguese seamen are rowed to safety from a ship wrecked off the African coast.

VICTORIA AND ALBERT MUSEUM

BIBLIOTHEQUE NATIONALE

LA CASA DE PORTUGAL

A SHIP FOR ROUNDING AFRICA

Prior to 1400 the typical European ship was an ungainly, one-masted tub that could do little more than spread its single sail and scud before the wind. The medieval Arab ship (left) was not much better for ocean voyaging, though light and easily driven. Gradually the Portuguese began to give their ships refinements, some of which are seen in the fifteenth-century bowl painting at upper left: to the barca*'s mainsail have been added small sails fore and aft that help her maneuver. Above is a model of Vasco da Gama's caravel, in which he sailed around Africa to India in 1497. It shows the advances that Portuguese shipbuilders had made by then: the square sails on the mainmast helped da Gama sail swiftly south before the prevailing breeze; the three aftermasts are rigged with lateen sails (so called because of their later prevalence in Latin countries) that let him tack home against the wind.*

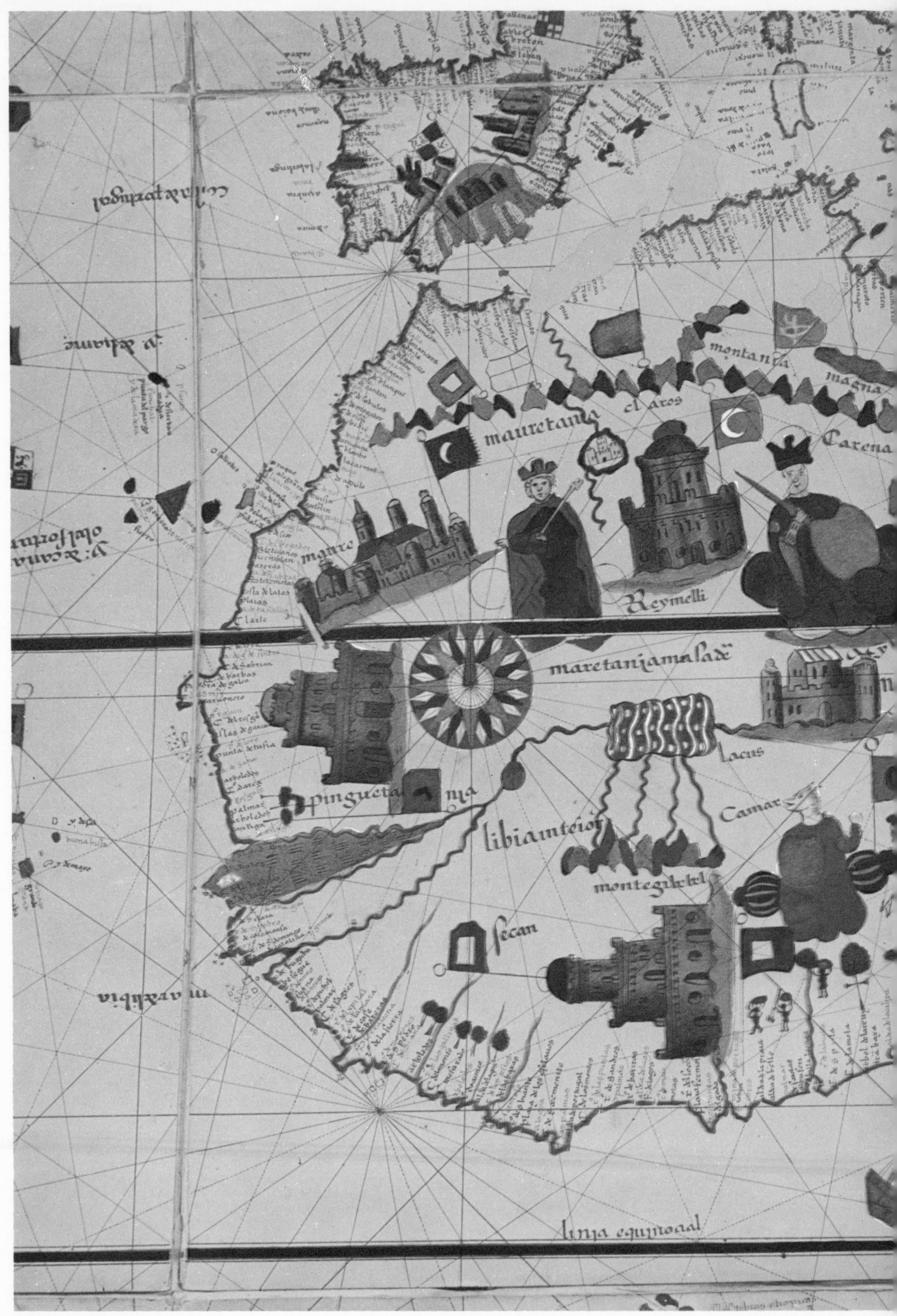

Juan de la Cosa, who became chart maker for Columbus, painted a map of Africa on oxhide. He pointed out Prester

N.Y. PUBLIC LIBRARY, MAP DIVISION

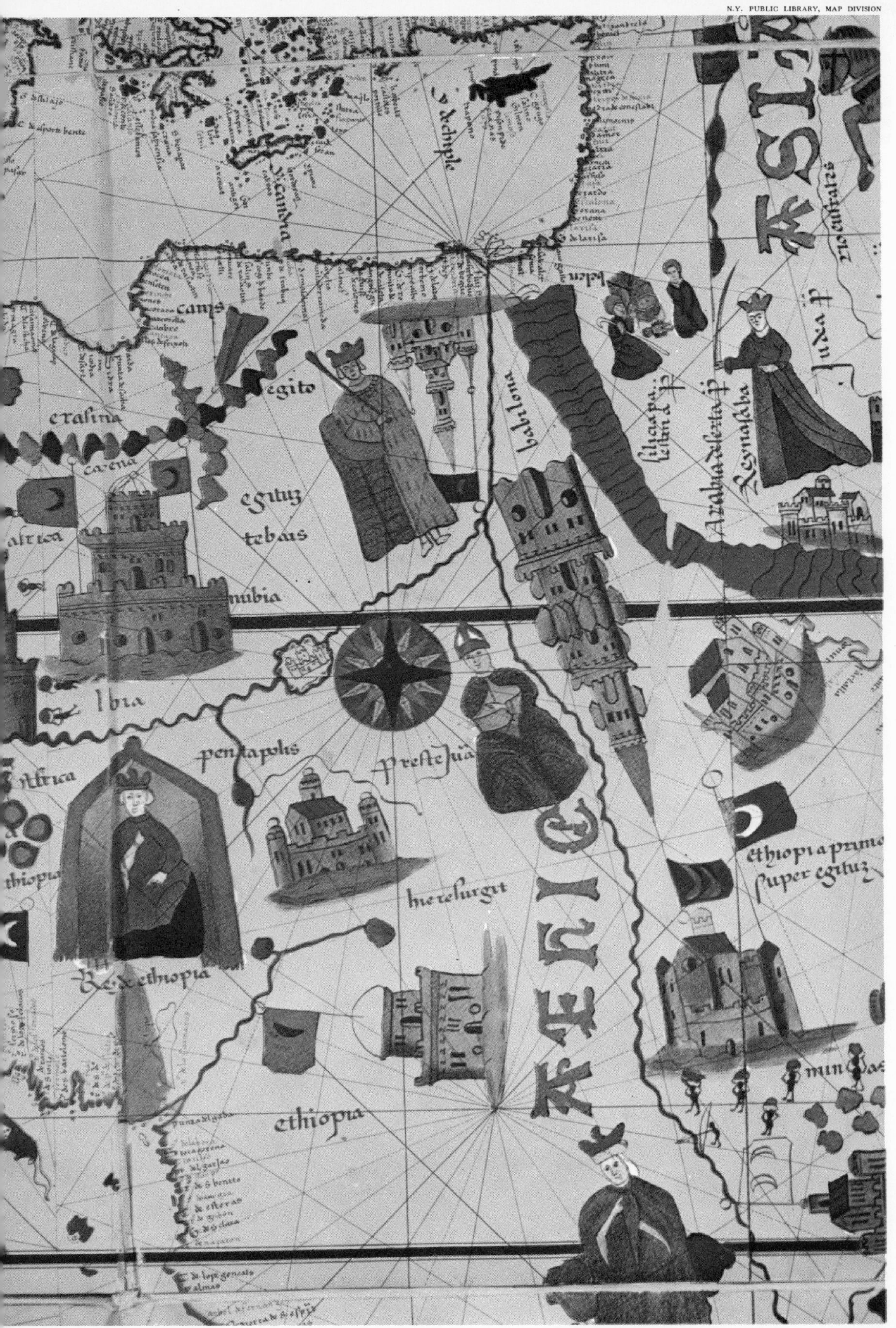

John's Ethiopian kingdom, just right of center, and drew the Niger so that it runs across the continent, joining the Nile.

This intricate ivory piece was carved by African artists who obviously regarded Portuguese explorers as hostile invaders.

TEXT CONTINUED FROM PAGE 32

Africa was indeed turning eastward toward the Orient, just as the Prince had hoped. He died believing that his captains had won a whole new continent for Portugal and were on their way to join Prester John.

It was not until 1493, when Pedro de Covilhão crossed the Red Sea from Arabia into Ethiopia, that the kingdom of Prester John was reached. But five years before that, in 1488, Bartholomew Dias discovered Africa's southernmost tip. Dias succeeded in this great feat by sailing around the bulge of West Africa into the gulf where the Niger's waters finally emerge, and down the coast past the mouth of the Congo. Then a great storm seized his two vessels and carried them south, out of sight of land, for thirteen days. At last the storm subsided and Dias turned east. But there was no land. In hope and wonder, he changed his course to north and finally landed at Mossel Bay. Dias wanted to continue sailing northeastward, but his fearful men forced him to return to Portugal.

When Dias appeared at court, he asserted that one could sail around Africa and beyond. But that honor—the first eastward passage past the Cape of Good Hope and northward along the coast of East Africa—went to Vasco da Gama. The voyage of da Gama was authorized by King Manuel the Fortunate, who had a rather different objective from his cousin Henry. Manuel was interested only in India, which he considered to be the world's greatest source of wealth. He instructed his captains to intensify their African explorations, for he certainly would not reject whatever riches that continent might yield; but he made it clear that the major purpose of voyaging south and east was to reach the Orient. Then Portugal, if she got there first, would command the vital sea route and be the most powerful nation in Europe.

Fortunately a diary survives of da Gama's amazing journey to India in 1497—although the Portuguese were not much better as record keepers than the Egyptians. The diary was of interest to later African explorers mainly because of its description of the coastal peoples and its warning of the ever-present possibility of sudden death on a distant shore. (See map on page 20.)

After sailing for four months, first southwest and then southeast, da Gama and his men came in sight of a land they did not recognize. After three days' further sailing, they entered St. Helena Bay, which lies just north of present-day Cape Town on the west coast of Africa. "In this land the men are swarthy," da Gama's diary noted. "They

BIBLIOTHEQUE NATIONALE, SERVICE PHOTOGRAPHIQUE

Vasco da Gama, the hardy captain who discovered Africa's southernmost tip, is seen in a conventional, courtly pose.

Description de l'Afrique, DAPPER, 1686

In 1482 the Portuguese put up this castle on the Guinea coast. It was a place to store goods as well as a fortress—and was named St. George, after the patron saint of Portugal.

eat only sea wolves and whales and the flesh of gazelles and the roots of plants . . . They have many dogs like those of Portugal and they bark the same as they do." A while later the men were attacked by the natives, one of the many such sad and bloody encounters between Africans and Europeans.

Da Gama resumed his voyage and rounded the Cape of Good Hope, entering Mossel Bay where Dias had been before him. Here on the beach the men erected a stone pillar with a cross on it, the symbol of Christianity and Portuguese sovereignty. But just as they were raising their sails to head northeastward, they saw a band of natives come out from the forest and knock the pillar over. Africa, the blacks' action seemed to say, would not be conquered that easily or in that generation.

As they followed the coast into the Indian Ocean, da Gama's men relied, when they could, on native pilots to guide them and to prepare them for new dangers. Da Gama found more and more signs that other men in swift ships had been there before him. These were Arabs, who had long held a trade monopoly in the area. When Mozambique's broad harbor was reached, the Portuguese were treated hospitably only because the natives assumed they must be Moslems too.

From Mozambique, the voyagers sailed for Mombasa, on the coast of Kenya. On the way they had a pitched battle with another band of Moslem traders who attacked the Portuguese when they drew into a small bay for water. Da Gama fought off the Moslems with the aid of the ships' bombards, or cannons, killing several and capturing two laden canoes. This fight was not caused by simple hostility or misunderstanding, as before. There was altogether too much understanding on both sides: if Vasco da Gama succeeded in establishing a trade route, Christianity would outflank Mohammedanism, and the Arab trade monopoly would be broken.

In Mombasa, which the Portuguese reached in April, 1498, their last native pilot escaped. Yet they were now eager to complete the last part of their journey to India, the passage across the Arabian Sea. The southwest monsoon was about to set in and it would take them straight to their goal. At last, in the town of Malindi, just one day's sail northeast of Mombasa, da Gama succeeded in capturing a high Moslem official and trading him for a pilot to guide them to the port of Calicut on the southwest coast of India. From that moment on, Europe had a direct trade route to the Far East.

Vasco da Gama, carrying out Prince Henry's design, had succeeded in charting large sections of the African coast. Henceforth the outlines of the continent would be known; and new explorers could dream of unlocking its interior secrets.

Fort Jesus in Mombasa kept resentful Arabs at bay for a generation after its completion in 1595. But when it fell, the Portuguese were gradually squeezed out of Africa.

PHOTO BY ROBERT S. KANE

III CONQUEST OF

The achievements of such men as da Gama, and the size and strength of his country's merchant fleet, won for Portugal the mastery of the seas around Africa. Portuguese dominance was threatened for the first time in 1553 when English merchants sailed to Morocco to barter cloth for ivory, gold, and pepper. But it was the Dutch, plunging into the African slave trade, who swept away the Portuguese monopoly of Africa late in the sixteenth century. Then, little more than a century later, the English finally emerged as the supreme foreign power in Africa. Victorious in 1815, at the close of the Napoleonic Wars, Great Britain was free to focus her attention on the vast unexplored regions of the Dark Continent.

By this time Mungo Park had already gone to Africa and had died while seeking the mouth of the Niger. Now the British proposed sending other expeditions to Africa to try and follow the river's course. In 1822 a government-sponsored expedition set out for Tripoli. Guiding it were a naval lieutenant named Hugh Clapperton and Major Dixon Denham, veteran of the wars against Napoleon.

The course they decided to follow took them across the Sahara and through the plains and grassy steppes of the Sudan. The perils of desert travel were many—not the least of them being the expected shortage of water. The men sometimes traveled three days without finding a well, stepping over the dried carcasses of men and animals that had preceded them and perished from thirst and fatigue.

And there were sandstorms too—so violent, Major Denham wrote, "as to fill the atmosphere and render the immense space before us impenetrable to the eye beyond a few yards." But they let nothing stop them. The Niger was their goal, and having come a great distance already, they could not bring themselves to turn back.

Their first target was not the Niger itself, but Lake Chad, which had long been thought to have some connec-

Clapperton, Denham, and their party approach a native community near Lake Chad. This picture is from a drawing Denham made for his book on Africa.

THE NIGER

Narrative of an Expedition, DENHAM, 1826

tion with the Niger. Perhaps the lake was the place where the Niger and Congo rivers met, for many people believed these rivers to be one and the same. Or perhaps the lake was the gateway to the rich cities that were believed to be strung out along Africa's water courses like pearls on a string.

Clapperton's party finally reached the lake in February, 1823, after traveling more than a thousand miles overland, which in itself was an extraordinary accomplishment. Denham wrote that upon seeing Lake Chad "my heart bounded within me . . . for I believed this lake to be the great object of our search."

Denham was destined for disappointment, as was his partner, for Lake Chad proved to have no connection with the Niger or with any of Africa's major river systems. How-

The explorers' camp at Lake Chad was set on low, grassy hills that overlooked a small native settlement.

Narrative of an Expedition, DENHAM, 1826

ever, since they were the first Europeans to have seen this body of water, they could take comfort in having made an important discovery.

The expedition was now in Bornu, a province of modern Nigeria, and on a March morning in 1823, the men were summoned for an audience with the region's portly sultan. According to Denham, they arrived in the sultan's court and saw his many subjects seated in a huge semicircle around his cagelike pavilion "with their backs to his royal person."

"Large bellies and large heads are indispensable for those who serve the court of Bornu," Denham wrote. And to meet these requirements, the natives padded their stomachs with wadding and wrapped their heads in enormous turbans of muslin or linen. "Nothing could be more ridiculous than the appearance of these people squatting down in their places, tottering under the weight and magnitude of their turbans and their bellies, while the thin legs that appeared underneath but ill accorded with the bulk of the other parts."

Denham (above) proved an excellent chronicler of the African journey he made with Clapperton (below).

Soon after visiting the sultan, the expedition split up, and Clapperton and some of his men set off toward the west, heading for the great Arab trading town of Kano. Denham, on the other hand, joined a group of friendly Bornu tribesmen and went south. It was a foolish move, for he quickly became involved in a savage skirmish between the natives he accompanied and a host of their enemies.

He watched in terror as enemy warriors literally butchered some of the men of his party. Would he receive the same treatment? As it happened, he did not. The warriors wounded him with their spears, but according to Denham "they were alone prevented from murdering me . . . I am persuaded, by the fear of injuring the value of my clothes, which appeared to them a rich booty." They tore his clothing from him, he recalled, and when they began to fight over it, "the idea of escape came like lightning across my mind, and without a moment's hesitation or reflection I crept underneath the belly of the horse nearest me and started as fast as my legs could carry me for the thickest part of the wood."

He eventually rejoined the tribesmen who had been his companions, and continued his journey. Unable to find the Niger, or any significant body of water, Denham returned north and explored the eastern shore of Lake Chad.

Clapperton, meanwhile, had not fared much better than his partner, for he had lost some important members of his

Narrative of an Expedition, DENHAM, 1826

Denham's journal describes at length his visit to the court of Bornu. He noted that although he got but a brief look at the sultan (left), he saw that "his turban was larger than any of his subjects' and . . . his face, from the nose downwards, was completely covered." Assembled before the sultan were his subjects (at right), some of whom wore as many as ten shirts to fill out the size of their bellies.

party and he himself had been weakened by a lingering fever. He was determined to reach Kano, however, for he had heard much about it during his travels. The town was the commercial center of the entire region that lay between Lake Chad and the Niger.

Clapperton showed the effects of his illness and of his long overland journey as he halted outside the city. The sun had burned his skin to a dark, brackish hue, and his face appeared wasted and gaunt. He rested under a tree, and after a good night's sleep prepared to enter the city the next day: January 20, 1824. He shed the dusty clothes he had been wearing and arrayed himself in his full-dress naval uniform. His high collar and still-gleaming gold buttons transformed him into a semblance of the strikingly tall, athletic Scotsman he had been at the outset of the journey.

Describing his arrival in Kano, Clapperton wrote: ". . . I had no sooner passed the gates than I felt grievously disappointed; for from the flourishing description of it given

Costume Antico e Moderno, FERRARIO, 1815

by the Arabs, I expected to see a city of surprising grandeur. I found, on the contrary, the houses nearly a quarter of a mile from the walls, and in many parts scattered into detached groups, between large and stagnant pools of water. I might have spared all the pains I had taken . . . for not an individual turned his head round to gaze at me, but all, intent on their own business, allowed me to pass by without notice or remark."

Clapperton could not have known it, but the citizens of Kano were used to seeing costumes far more splendid than his. For every day, traders from the Eastern Sudan, the Gold Coast, and regions as far north as the Mediterranean poured through the gates of the city. Clapperton developed a liking for Kano. He remained there a full month, enjoying the bustling markets and the ceremonial boxing matches. Then he went on to Sokoto, where he boldly initiated conversations with Sultan Bello, one of the most influential rulers of West Africa. At first the talks went well, for Clapperton was both a good talker and a

At the desert town of Musfeia, a shower of arrows, shot from behind a "strong fence of palisades, well pointed," greeted Denham and his companions.

good listener. But at the second meeting he made the mistake of saying that the people and the government of Britain wished the slave trade to be discontinued. He should have known that the sultan derived most of his income from the capture and sale of slaves and that he would fight to the death any attempt to cut off that important source of revenue. It was perhaps because of Clapperton's unfortunate slip of the tongue that he was not permitted to proceed to the Niger, only 150 miles away. Disappointed, he turned back and met Denham near Lake Chad. They arrived in England in June, 1825, their mission unfulfilled.

Despite this failure, the British government did not lose interest. The demand for more knowledge about the possibilities for trade in West Africa made it necessary that the Niger mystery be solved. The use of the river as an avenue for trade could be decided only when its entire course was finally charted. Clapperton was promoted to the rank of commander and awarded a commission from the Secretary for War and the Colonies to lead another expedition to the interior—this time from the coast of West Africa.

The commander had four British companions with him this time—but not for long. Two of them died soon after leaving their base camp on the coast near the present-day border between Nigeria and Dahomey. A third member of the group decided to strike out on his own. So, early in the journey, Clapperton was left with but one of his countrymen, his twenty-one-year-old servant, Richard Lander.

Lander had traveled widely, despite his youth. Since leaving school at the age of thirteen, he had served many masters on voyages to various parts of Europe and to the West Indies and South Africa. And it was Africa, more than any other land, that appealed to his romantic spirit. Sometime later he was to write that "there was a charm in the very sound of 'Africa' that always made my heart flutter on hearing it mentioned."

Together Clapperton and Lander led their retinue toward Busa, the town where Mungo Park was presumed to have died. They reached the Niger in the spring of 1826 and proceeded along the route that Clapperton had tried to follow once before. Gradually they made their way to Kano and then to Sokoto, where Clapperton hoped to reopen discussions with Sultan Bello. Britain was eager to conclude a trade agreement with the powerful ruler, and Clapperton was determined not to fail in bringing it about.

However, when Clapperton reached the sultan's camp, he found the potentate wholly committed to war and only remotely interested in entering into negotiations with any foreign power. Clapperton resolved to be patient and remain near Sokoto until it was advantageous for him to have a long, and hopefully fruitful, talk with the sultan.

Then on March 12, 1827, Clapperton suffered an attack of dysentery. It was left to Lander to care for him, which proved a supreme test of his loyalty as a servant, and of his devotion. In his journal, Lander wrote: "From the moment he was first taken ill, Captain Clapperton perspired freely, large drops of sweat continually rolling over every part of his body . . . and being unable to obtain anyone, even of our own servants, to assist, I was obliged to wash the clothes, kindle and keep in the fire, and prepare the victuals with my own hands. Owing to the intense heat, my master was frequently fanned for hours together; indeed all my leisure moments were devoted to this tedious occupation; and I have often held the fan till, from excessive weakness, it has fallen from my grasp."

Nearly a month passed, and during that time, Lander reported that "[Clapperton] was gradually but perceptibly

Record of Captain Clapperton, CLAPPERTON, 1830

Wearing a turban and a well-trimmed beard, Richard Lander looked more like a sultan than a servant. This picture is from the journal of Clapperton's last expedition, published in 1830.

declining; his body, from being strong and vigorous, having become exceedingly weak and emaciated, and indeed little better than a skeleton. There could not be a more truly pitiable object in the universe than was my poor dear master at this time. . . ."

On the morning of April 13, Lander awoke to the sound of Clapperton's loud breathing. He saw his master struggling to get to his feet, a wild expression on his face. Lander ran to him. Then, the young servant stated, "I clasped him in my arms, and whilst I thus held him, could feel his heart palpitating violently. His throes became every moment less vehement, and at last they entirely ceased." Clapperton fell back, dead.

"I held the lifeless body in my arms . . . overwhelmed with grief," wrote Lander. ". . . oh God, what was my distress in that agonizing moment! . . . I flung myself along the bed of death and prayed that Heaven would in mercy take my life."

Lander's grief did not sway him from his mission, however; as his master had requested, he retrieved Clapperton's papers and delivered them back to England. He wrote an account of his adventures which was published along with Clapperton's journal in 1829.

But Lander's career in Africa was far from over. He was only twenty-five, and a very persuasive man despite the humbleness apparent in his writings. The fact that he was a servant did not deter him from prevailing upon the government to send him to Africa in an attempt to trace the Niger from Busa to its mouth.

He finally received backing for his expedition, but it was a paltry amount—only a hundred pounds—hardly enough to take care of his needs or those of his brother John, whom he intended to take along. The Landers reached Dahomey on March 22, 1830, and arrived at Busa on June 17. Three months later, when they had hired some native helpers, they set out on their great adventure down the Niger's sluggish current.

At a village called Bocqua, midway between Busa and the sea, the Landers and their men left the boats and climbed ashore to rest. But their relaxation was interrupted by one of the men who rushed into camp, screaming in terror that some natives were about to attack them. Lander wrote that he then saw "a large party of men, almost naked, running . . . toward our encampment. They were all variously armed with muskets, bows and arrows, knives, . . . long spears, and other instruments of destruction."

Lander and his men gathered up their muskets and pistols, but he was determined to avoid bloodshed—for one important reason: he knew his party was outnumbered and could neither win a battle with these natives nor escape from them. Lander ordered his men not to fire unless they were fired on first, and the group stood fast.

The natives were advancing swiftly now, and Lander noticed that one of them, who appeared to be the chief, was walking ahead of the others. Richard and John threw down their pistols and calmly walked toward him.

"As we approached him," wrote Richard Lander, "we made all the signs and motions we could with our arms to deter him and his people from firing on us. His quiver was dangling at his side, his bow was bent, and an arrow which was pointed at our breasts already trembled on the string when we were within a few yards of his person. This was a highly critical moment—the next might be our last. But the hand of Providence averted the blow; for just as the chief was about to pull the fatal cord, a man that was nearest him rushed forward and stayed his arm. At that instant we stood before him and immediately held forth our hands; all of them trembled like aspen leaves. The chief looked up full in our faces . . . his body was convulsed all over, as though he were enduring the utmost torture . . . he drooped his head, eagerly grasped our proffered hands, and burst into tears. This was a sign of friendship—harmony followed, and war and bloodshed were thought of no more."

The Landers were fortunate that time, but a bit farther downstream their good fortune ran out. About fifty native canoes were sighted coming toward them; some had the British Union Jack mounted on bamboo poles, and sewed to some other flags were figures of men's legs and of chairs, tables, decanters, and glasses. The people in the canoes were dressed as Europeans except that they did not wear trousers. In that part of the country, only chiefs were allowed to have trousers.

At first Richard Lander was overjoyed at the sight of these people—until he noticed that they were pointing muskets at him. There was no chance to stage a successful fight or to flee. The Lander brothers were seized, their supplies and clothing stolen, and soon they learned that they were to be handed over as prisoners to the ruler of a region nearby. But when they were brought to that ruler's court, they were ransomed by another ruler, named King Boy, who hoped to get an even higher price for the two foreigners at the coast.

Journal of an Expedition . . . , LANDER, 1832

The Landers were fooled at first by the British insignia on the flags flying from this canoe. But they found out, as the canoe came nearer, that the boatmen were natives—the fiercest Niger tribesmen they would meet.

BOTH: BALTIMORE MUSEUM OF ART, WURTZBURGER COLLECTION

The Benin, Bakota, and Ibo tribes once had thriving cultures in Central Africa, near the mouth of the Niger. The warrior above is by an artist of the Benin tribe, which is known for its bronze sculpture. The Ibo death mask at right was used at funerals. The wearer, dressed in bright colors, was supposed to use a voice like the deceased's.

The bronze rooster above, product of Benin's advanced civilization, is more realistic but no less artistic than the Bakota figure (left) that represents a dead spirit.

But neither of the brothers despaired. They endured their privations patiently, in much the way of Mungo Park. Soon they were brought to the coastal town of Brass, and King Boy proceeded to bargain with the captain of the English brig *Thomas* for custody of John and Richard Lander.

The captain of the brig succeeded in getting both brothers on board and kicking off King Boy without paying him a penny of the promised ransom money. After spending a terrifying time while the vessel tried to sail out across a sand bar—with the natives waiting grimly on the shore for a shipwreck—the Landers felt the salt air in their faces and knew that at last their terrible journey was over. It had been arduous, but it had been a success. The brothers arrived in England with the definite information that the Niger came down to the sea in the Gulf of Guinea. They had won for their country one of Africa's most sought-after prizes.

OVERLEAF: *A nineteenth-century Italian artist, Giulio Ferrario, painted a watercolor of an elaborate festival he attended in a native village near the Niger.*

Costume Antico e Moderno, FERRARIO, 1815

L'Afrique, LYONS, 1821

IV TO TIMBUCTOO

Lieutenant Hugh Clapperton, leading an official British expedition, was the first European in modern times to cross the Sahara. His route on the map (page 20) looks like the only sensible way for a European to get to the Negro lands of West Africa above the Gulf of Guinea: it leads directly south from the Mediterranean port of Tripoli. But in fact the route is the most perilous in Africa, as later explorers found.

The Sahara, which stretches completely across North Africa, three thousand miles from the Atlantic to the Nile, looks from the air like the face of a burned-out planet. But it is by no means dead or featureless. Mountains as lofty as eleven thousand feet thrust up from valleys no higher than sea level, and here and there are oases large enough and fertile enough to support sizeable cities. The most commonly held misconception about the world's greatest desert is that it is all sand. Actually the rippled sand dunes, which are found mostly in the region directly below the Atlas Mountains, take up only one seventh of the Sahara's total area.

Two other parts of the Sahara give a better idea of the great desert's variety—and its hostility. They are the Ahaggar range, which has been called the mountain heart of the Sahara, and the Tanezrouft plain, which has all the beauty of an endless, uninhabited parking lot. In the Ahaggar Mountains live the proudest of the six Tuareg tribes. Here they have been able to keep their strange language and ancient customs unchanged; among these wild gorges and wind-eroded peaks they have retreated after raiding the rich oases at the desert's fringe. The Tanezrouft has also served as a haven for fugitives—its shale-covered surface is so rough that no foot leaves a trace—but no man by himself can stand its monotonous loneliness for long without going mad.

Yet it was through the Tanezrouft region that René

TEXT CONTINUED ON PAGE 62

The swirling, stinging fury of a Sahara sandstorm was drawn by an Englishman named George F. Lyons, who made an attempt to cross the desert in 1818.

In a book about his experiences in the Sahara, Lyons included this drawing of a band of Arabs on training maneuvers

L'Afrique, LYONS, 1821

Armed with lances and muskets, they remained in constant readiness to defend their communities or raid their enemies.

Le Voyage de Rene Caillie, CAILLIE, 1830

René Caillié, who traveled with Moslems crossing the desert, wears a native costume in this engraving.

TEXT CONTINUED FROM PAGE 59

Caillié traveled, the next European after Clapperton to cross the Sahara and live to tell of it. Caillié's objective was Timbuctoo. He wanted to be the first Westerner to reach the city whose existence, despite its position as the hub of the Sahara's caravan traffic, was then only a rumor outside Africa.

Of all the nineteenth-century explorers of Africa, Caillié seemed the least likely to succeed. He was poor, uneducated, skilled in neither science nor language, totally without influence, not robust, and so unprepossessing that he had difficulty commanding an audience even after his great accomplishments were known. The one quality that led him through his adventures was an incredible will to see and to overcome Africa.

Caillié was born in the French village of Mauzé in 1799, the sixth child of an impoverished baker. Even his youth was occupied by thoughts of exploration. "All my spare time," he wrote later, "was taken up with books of travel. The map of Africa, which so far as I could see showed only desert or unexplored regions, fired my imagination above all others." By the time he was sixteen he had narrowed the focus of his imagination to Timbuctoo. Determined to reach that legendary ancient city, he set out from his native village with but a few personal possessions in his knapsack and sixty francs (about twelve dollars) in his pocket.

Caillié reached the coast of Africa, but no farther. A second attempt three years later also failed, although he did succeed in getting malaria. The determined Frenchman was twenty-five when he came to Africa for the third time, and his plans were considerably more mature. He intended to disguise himself as a Moslem, reach Timbuctoo by way of the Niger River, then cross the totally unexplored western part of the Sahara to Tangier. Setting off from the coast of Senegal, he walked without stopping until he found a native tribe willing to let him live among them and learn their language. He ate the food, wore the clothes, and endured the hardships of these Arabic-speaking Negro Bedouins. But their tolerance never reached the point of civility; he was never afforded any privacy. And no matter how often he repeated their Mohammedan prayers with them or how patiently he bore their rudeness, Caillié was always regarded as a freakish animal. He endured it for a year.

In the Persian miniature at right, a Moslem caravan laden with gifts moves eastward on a pilgrimage to Mecca, the birthplace of the prophet Mohammed.

و فرزین میشود و پیادگان حاج بادیه بسر بردند و بتر شدند
از من بگوی حاجی مردم گزای را
کو پوستین خلق بآزار میدرد

Journal d'un Voyage a Temboctou et a Jenne, CAILLIE, 1830

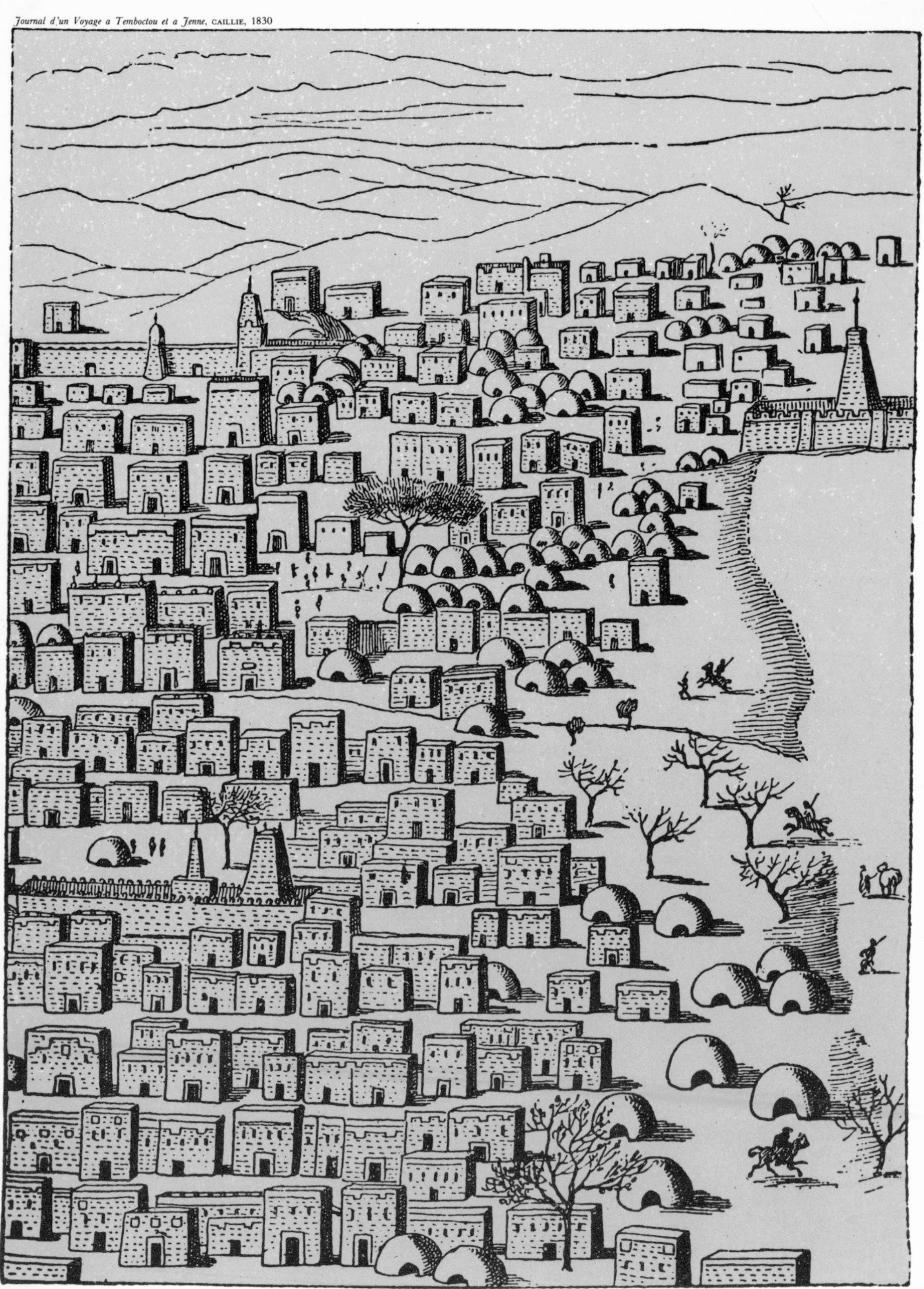

Then, after working an additional year at an English post to earn more money, he started at last for Timbuctoo. It was April 19, 1827, when he left the coast. Caillié's determination was reinforced by news that the Geographical Society of Paris had offered a ten-thousand-franc reward to any Frenchman who succeeded in bringing back a first-hand report from that city. As a precaution he had prepared a story that he considered believable enough to insure a friendly reception from natives along the way. He said that he had been born in Egypt of Arab parents and as a baby had been taken to France by Napoleon's army; now he was trying to return to the land of his birth by way of Timbuctoo.

Caillié joined a small native caravan heading into the interior, and he was relieved to find that his story was accepted by tribesmen along the route. Apparently his knowledge of Mohammedan law calmed the suspicions aroused by his white skin. Yet he was pestered and robbed, once by the leader of his own caravan; Caillié made no complaint. He and his companions kept on at a fierce pace—traveling without a break from six in the morning until midafternoon—and thus they arrived on the upper Niger in less than two months. But it was still some distance to Timbuctoo, and the brutality of the journey was beginning to affect the young Frenchman.

The first sign of this was a hideous sore on Caillié's foot; then he became afflicted with scurvy. Finally the caravan abandoned him and he underwent "incredible suffering," praying unashamedly for death. But in the hut of a kindly native he finally recovered and was able to proceed again.

Caillié completed the last five hundred miles of his journey on a primitive cargo boat going down the Niger. The Moslems still believed his story and treated him fairly well. However, as he was almost without funds, he was forced to sleep on the open deck and share the food of slaves who were being transported downriver. At dawn on April 20, 1828, he entered Timbuctoo. He recorded his first reaction: "I have never felt a similar emotion, and my transport was extreme. I was obliged, however, to restrain my feelings, and to God alone did I confide my joy."

A closer look at the town was a letdown for Caillié.

TEXT CONTINUED ON PAGE 68

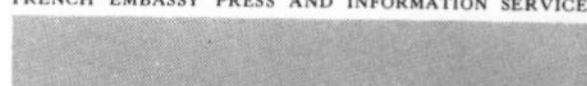
FRENCH EMBASSY PRESS AND INFORMATION SERVICE

In the photograph above of a modern Sahara village, the houses resemble the structures that Caillié drew in 1828 after he arrived in Timbuctoo (left).

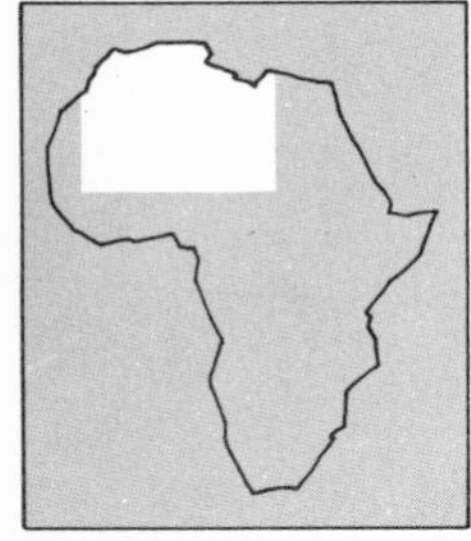

THE SAHARA OF IBN BATUTA

Moving easily on camels over sand and wasteland (below) where Europeans penetrated only at peril of their lives, Arab traders have always been the most successful travelers in Saharan Africa. Outstanding among them was ibn Batuta, whose early travels took him from Tangier across the great desert to the east coast of Africa, and thence overland to India and Southeast Asia. Astride his camel, like the fourteenth-century Arab at right, ibn Batuta could cover two hundred desert miles in a week. He reached Timbuctoo in 1353 and wrote of the Niger, "It cannot be visited by any white man because [the natives] would kill him before he got there." Before then, some of the Arabs' geographical knowledge had been passed on to the West by the famous cartographer Idrisi. The Sahara section of his 1154 map, shown below at right, is turned so that north appears at the top—it roughly conforms to the insert at left. In the lower right corner of the map is the fountain that Idrisi believed to be the common source of both the Nile River and the Niger River.

FRENCH EMBASSY PRESS AND INFORMATION SERVICE

BIBLIOTHEQUE NATIONALE

N.Y. PUBLIC LIBRARY, MAP DIVISION

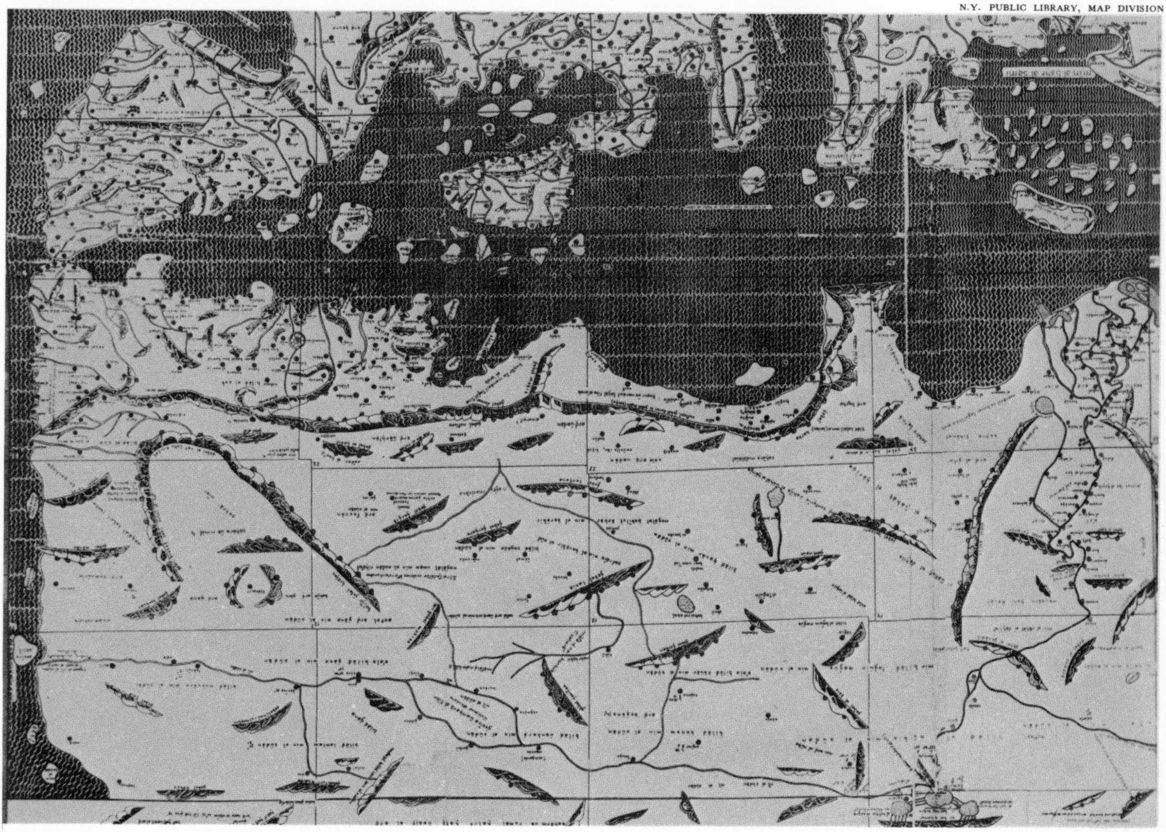

TEXT CONTINUED FROM PAGE 65

"The city presented . . . nothing but a mass of ill-looking houses built of earth. Nothing was to be seen in all directions but immense plains of quicksand of a yellowish-white color. The sky was a pale red as far as the horizon." On further inspection, Caillié found that some of the inhabitants lived comfortably enough. However, none were free from the threat of violence, for the city was constantly menaced by the Tuaregs, masters of the Sahara that stretched beyond the dazzling horizon to the north.

The North African merchants of Timbuctoo welcomed Caillié, and he was lodged in a house near the marketplace. But he was miserable, for this was not the city he had yearned to find. After traveling an entire year to get there, he stayed only two weeks.

On May 4, 1828, he left with a caravan of six-hundred camels and headed across the western Sahara. His course was much farther west than Clapperton's 1823 route and was roughly parallel to it. Caillié's caravan started into the unrelieved heat and monotony of the Tanezrouft, where several days' journey separated each meager well. Gradually conditions worsened. Once in a sandstorm, blinded and lost, he was sure he would die. But he and the other scattered parts of the great caravan re-formed and started on again. Weeks passed and the men of the caravan became increasingly hostile. In the middle of the Sahara they forced Caillié to dismount from his camel. He walked the rest of the way, suffering all the indignities and the privations of a slave. He called the experience—the stonings and beatings and bedevilings—"a martyrdom infinitely worse than death."

HACHETTE

A black-veiled Tuareg and his servant share a camel's durable back.

After three months of traveling through unmapped desert, Caillié dared strike out on his own when the Atlas Mountains came into sight. But the Moroccan territory that he still had to pass through to reach the port city of Tangier was forbidden to foreigners. A Christian would be killed immediately if he was caught. Proceeding cautiously by night, Caillié finally reached Fez, where a representative of the French government would not let him hide or rest—the man could not be convinced that this bundle of rags and sunburned skin begging for aid was really a civilized European. So he continued on to the north and made it to Tangier, on the Strait of Gibraltar, on September 7. There he found a consul who recognized him as a European, and who, after hearing the traveler's story, realized the importance of his achievement. Caillié had covered more than 2,800 miles in 538 days. When he finally returned to

Paris, he was received as a hero. He was made a chevalier of the Legion of Honor and was toasted at a special meeting of the Geographical Society of Paris.

Caillié achieved what he had set out to do, but his health was ruined and his spirit broken. Laboriously he completed the report of his journey, which the people of Paris very quickly came to doubt. They too had expected more of Timbuctoo—and they challenged his description of it. For all his relentless courage, Caillié remained an amateur explorer; he did not have the skill or the temperament to give a scientifically accurate account of what he had seen. Many people began to doubt that he had actually reached Timbuctoo. Even the government came to regard him less respectfully, and eventually it denied him a part of his promised pension. He died in 1838, forgotten and impoverished, at the age of thirty-nine.

It was left to a German—and a wholly different kind of explorer—to salvage Caillié's reputation.

In London in 1850, preparations were being made to outfit the English Mixed Scientific and Commercial Expedition. Because of the travels of Clapperton and Caillié, the extent and the value of the desert territories between the Mediterranean and the Niger were beginning to be realized. But many questions remained: What were the risks and dangers for a European nation that wanted to control the area? The British government recognized that exploration of the most thorough sort was necessary if the answers were to be found.

Having only recently returned from Africa, James Richardson was the obvious man to lead this new British effort. The experience he had gained reconnoitering the Sahara slave routes for English missionary societies fitted him perfectly for the assignment. But Richardson could not find men of sufficient scientific skill or interest in either Britain or France. It was only when he was introduced to Dr. Heinrich Barth, a philosopher and geographer of Hamburg, that he felt he had found a companion of proper devotion.

The scholarly Dr. Barth soon proved himself to be the most able man of the expedition, in part because of his tolerance. The route of the expedition skirted around the Ahaggar Mountains and passed through a region of which nothing was known in Europe—nothing except that an Arab traveler named ibn Batuta had been through it in the fourteenth century. Once, Richardson and Barth came upon a caravan of slave traders, all of whom had been

PHOTO SOCIETE GEOGRAPHIE, PARIS

Dr. Barth, a meticulous man down to the cut of his whiskers, was not a dreamer like Caillié; he was recognized as a highly gifted scientist.

murdered by marauding tribesmen from the mountains. Then they too were stopped by an onrush of Tuaregs. They were released only after one third of their goods had been taken; Barth commented merely that the expedition should not have aroused the natives' cupidity by taking so many supplies.

After crossing the Sahara from north to south, the party reached Lake Chad toward the beginning of 1851. There Richardson died, another victim of Africa's murderous climate. Left on his own, Barth decided to continue the journey and carry out his mission by adapting himself completely to African ways. He donned the long robes of an Arab and learned the language of the natives in the Chad area. He called himself Abd el Kerim, "Servant of the Lord," but he did not do so to deceive the natives—nor, with his great blond beard, could he have passed as an African if he had wanted to. He hoped, rather, to stay among the natives and study them, trying to understand their philosophy by steeping himself in it.

He wandered through the once-mighty Sudanese kingdoms near Lake Chad and made his headquarters on the lake's western shore. By his honesty and energy he even won the respect of the local sultan. His own supplies having long since given out, he lived on the kindness of the sultan of Bornu for several months. At length, in September, 1852, a packet from England reached him with a letter recognizing him as head of the expedition and ordering him to proceed to Timbuctoo.

When Barth reached Timbuctoo, more than a thousand miles west of Lake Chad, he saw that everything was essentially as Caillié had claimed; he vowed that the Frenchman would get the credit for having been there first. However, his reaction to the town differed from his predecessor's. To Barth, Timbuctoo was not the drab collection of mud huts that had so depressed Caillié, but an enormously rich storehouse of research possibilities.

Despite his enjoyment of the city, Barth came near to death in Timbuctoo—first by illness, then at the hands of a fanatic in the sultan's court who wanted to kill him. But at last he was well enough to leave, and after traveling for ten months on the Niger and overland, he reached Lake Chad again in January of 1855. By this time he was close to starvation; he was diseased, and oppressed by loneliness. But his courage revived when he heard of Europeans in a nearby village. Scarcely believing his eyes when he saw an English and a German flag flying in the distance, he fell into the arms of three white men who came forth to greet him. The men, led by a young German named Eduard Vogel, had been sent out by the British government to look for Barth. As delighted as they all were to see one another, none of them were particularly surprised to have accomplished such a feat. The age of African exploration was indeed advancing to the point where the paths of European explorers might be expected to cross.

Barth returned to Europe by an easterly route through the desert. His five-volume journal, *Travels in Africa*, became mandatory reading for those who journeyed after him—traders, soldiers, and administrators. It not only described Saharan and sub-Saharan Africa with a professional accuracy that adventurers like Park and Caillié could never have achieved but set forth guidelines for safe passage through the continent. Be deliberate, the book urged future explorers, and have the ability to await results patiently.

Years later, when he was advising a young protégé who was on the point of leaving for Africa, Barth said, "The best weapon for the Christian traveler in Africa is decency —impeccable decency—toward the natives." If his words had been remembered, the history of African development might not have been as bloodstained and tragic as it was.

This lithograph is from a drawing Barth made of a procession to the sultan of Bornu's palace. Awaiting fresh supplies, Barth had to live off the sultan's generosity.

Travels in Central Africa, BARTH, 1857

V

THE FEHR COLLECTION, CAPE TOWN

THE GREAT TREK

The exploration of South Africa had a totally different character from that of any other part of the continent. The magnificent region that lies north of the Cape of Good Hope was to be explored and opened up not by isolated and courageous individuals, but by a lusty and expansive young nation.

Though Portuguese explorers and traders had been back and forth around the Cape ever since the end of the fifteenth century, they had little use for the area except as a station for getting fresh supplies of food and water for their ships. Their real interest lay in their colonies on the west and east coasts of Africa and in India.

In 1648, however, the Dutch sailing ship *Haarlem* was wrecked near the Cape of Good Hope, and the crew had to live there for nearly a year before they were rescued. Largely because of their enthusiastic descriptions of the climate, the rich soil, and the rivers that flowed without ceasing, the Dutch East India Company sent three ships to the Cape in 1652 under the command of Jan van Riebeeck. He was instructed to establish a station that would supply water, vegetables, and meat to company ships en route to and from India. Water was plentiful enough, but food was more difficult to obtain, and from time to time, the Dutch East India Company had to send supplies to the settlers. But gradually, van Riebeeck and his people began to plant gardens, learned to hunt successfully, and even traded with the natives for cattle and sheep. Although the colony was not a complete success as a way station, the settlers had established a foothold on the Cape.

Then in 1684 more pioneers were sent out from Holland, and shortly afterward a group of refugees from religious persecution in France arrived at the Cape. Almost all of these settlers, however, became discontented with the rule of the Dutch East India Company, and as the colonists prospered, they began to explore and settle farther in-

Dutch settlers fight off a Bantu raid during their arduous trek beyond the Orange River. Their wagons are similar to those used by American pioneers.

land where they hoped to find a measure of independence.

This was the start of that tremendous movement in South African history known as trekking, a migration that paralleled in many ways the opening up of the American West. The geography of the two regions was similar, for the inland territories of South Africa were nearly as vast as those of America. From the Cape it was 1,250 miles to the Zambezi River, and though the sprawling Kalahari Desert occupied the west-central part of the area, there were millions of square miles of uplands that had a temperate climate and were well suited for farming and cattle raising.

In some districts, grazing land had to be taken by force from the natives, who also raised cattle, just as the pioneers in America later took land from the Indians. This violence, whites against blacks, was precisely what Barth had warned against. It is often forgotten, however, that many natives themselves were engaged in conquest.

In fact, a great wave of Bantu tribes were advancing from the north at almost the same time as Dutch farmers—called Boers—were moving up from the south. The only

Johannes Schumacher painted this watercolor of the sprawling settlement of Cape Town in 1775, little more than a hundred years after its founding. Behind the colony is the lofty flat peak of Table Mountain.

long-time inhabitants of this land were the Hottentots and the Bushmen, the nomadic hunters of South Africa.

As in America, riches other than farmland began to attract the settlers. At first no one suspected the existence of the gold and diamonds that were found later in South Africa, but as early as 1681 tribesmen from the west arrived at the Cape with samples of copper ore which they had dug from a mountain near them. Word began to spread of the easily obtainable mineral riches. In August of 1685 the governor of the Cape, Simon van der Stel, decided to lead an expedition to find the source of the ore.

After slogging through swamps and rattling over rocky hills on which a number of their wagons and carts were wrecked, van der Stel and his company reached the Copper Mountains on October 21, 1685. "The mountains were colored from top to bottom with verdigris [copper carbonate]," they noted with joy. The men built smelting furnaces, and at last after several disappointments, obtained copper.

These pioneers of South Africa were practical explorers

THE FEHR COLLECTION, CAPE TOWN

Jan van Riebeeck, who appears in this seventeenth-century woodcut, founded the Cape colony in 1652.

H.A.M. SWELLENGREBEL COLLECTION, BREDA, NETHERLANDS

SOUTH AFRICAN MUSEUM, CAPE TOWN

Dutch flags fly over Governor van der Stel's camp in the Copper Mountains. Hendrick Claudius, who drew this picture, went with the governor's party to search for the rich lode of copper they had been told was in the mountains.

who penetrated the interior to find a livelihood for themselves and their families. They were not concerned with the triumphs of discovery; they had come to conquer, and to stay. The new land was as rich as it was beautiful, and they intended to prosper on it.

At the beginning of the eighteenth century, the Cape colony had a population of about ten thousand. A hundred years later, it was well over twenty-five thousand and growing fast. After the wars between Britain and Holland at the end of the eighteenth and the beginning of the nineteenth century, the Cape passed to British rule. Dutch was still the official language, and at first the Boers were quite pleased with the change; they no longer had to live under the commercial restrictions of the Dutch East India Company. But some years later, when the British passed laws for the protection of African slaves, the Boers began to grumble.

Then in 1834 the British outlawed slavery completely. Further, they gave support to the Bantu tribesmen, who had been the main source of slaves. These two actions, which intensified the Boers' desire to leave the Cape area, were the causes of the Great Trek that began in 1835.

The object of this movement was to penetrate the unknown region beyond the Orange River, thus escaping beyond British control. By 1837, about two thousand persons had crossed the river and settled in a number of camps on the other side. This hardly seems a large number, but the Boers were astonishingly prolific people.

The trekkers beyond the Orange River elected a governor, Piet Retief, a descendant of one of the old settler families and a man of education and talent. Retief saw that although the Boers had found freedom on the high, open plains of the interior, they now faced the possibility of being cut off from the civilized world. He determined to lead as many of his independent-minded people as would follow him across the Drakensberg Mountains into the coastal area of Natal, even though some British traders had already settled there.

It took Retief's men two months to drag wagons over the mountains and down again. Often they had to dismantle the heavy carts and carry them piece by piece through crevasses and along boulder-strewn trails. On the way, also, there was constant danger from wild animals—not so much to the people themselves as to their livestock, which was their livelihood. Only by becoming machines themselves, forcing one another beyond the bounds of normal human endurance, could they survive the journey

TEXT CONTINUED ON PAGE 82

An Englishman named Awnsham Churchill, who traveled to South Africa in the eighteenth century, drew as many indigenous creatures as he could into this outdoor scene. In the text that accompanied his drawing,

Collection of Voyages, CHURCHILL, 1746

the artist pointed out the coconut palms, the "tyger" entering a wooden trap, the tribesmen closing in on an antelope, and a large reptile (left foreground) that he believed was either a crocodile or an alligator.

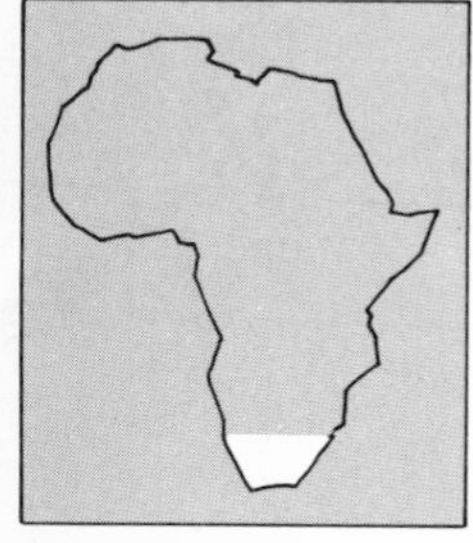

THE BOERS' SOUTH AFRICA

South Africa was regarded as little more than a navigational hazard by the early voyagers bound for India. Europeans suspected neither the region's mineral wealth nor its cultural riches (such as the superb prehistoric cave painting at bottom right). Thus the first Dutch ships to round the Cape of Good Hope, pictured on the 1598 map below, sailed eastward without stopping. But later ships did stop, and in 1652 a settlement was established on the Cape. The interior was not opened up until the Boers, a breed of self-sufficient Dutch farmers, began their Great Trek in 1835. Inland they found a dry, mountainous land. Part of the region, which they called the High Veldt, was green much of the year, bearing lush growth (right). Some Boers stayed in the veldt, where they had to overcome native tribesmen; others forced their wagons over the Drakensberg Mountains and down to the coastal plain of Natal ("Terra do Natall" on the map); and still others trekked into the unexplored areas to the north and northwest. This rugged, ruthless pioneering by an entire people, which was so unlike the exploration and development of the rest of Africa, has much to do with the extreme nationalism of present-day South Africa.

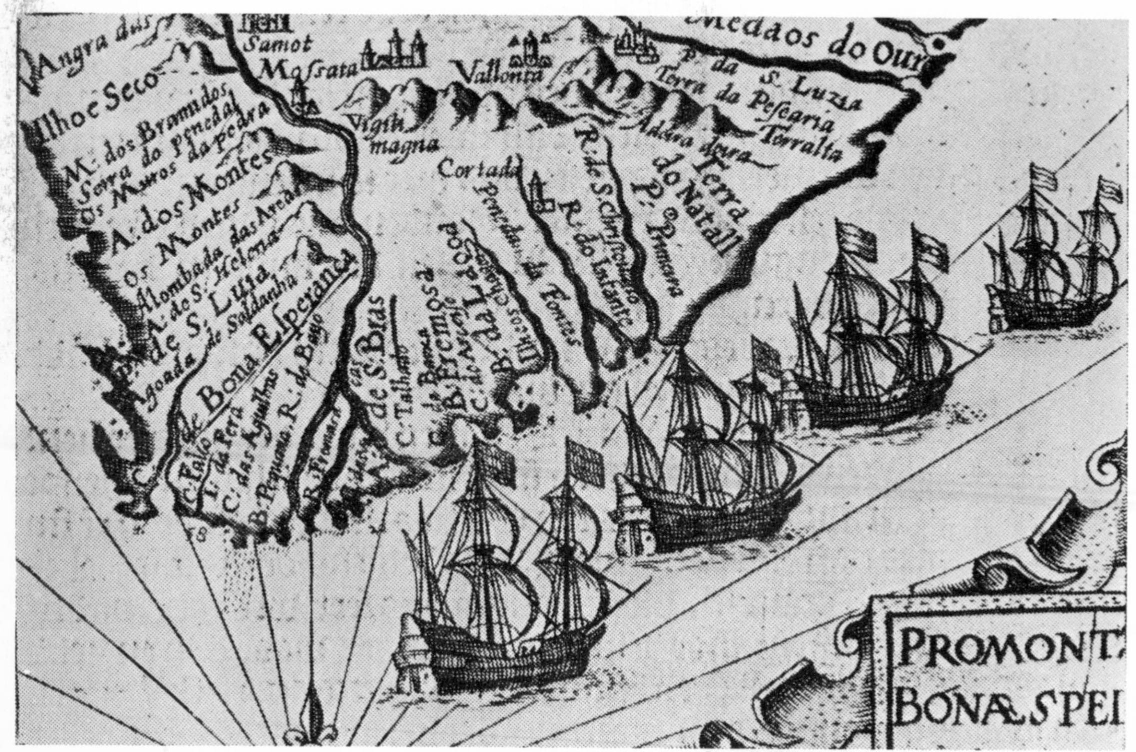

Diarum Nauticum Itineris Batavorum in Indiam Orientalem, AMSTERDAM, 1598

SOUTH AFRICAN TOURIST CORPORATION

Bushmen Paintings, TONGUE, COURTESY CLARENDON PRESS, OXFORD

1838

Know all men by this that Whereas
Pieter Retief Governor of the dutch Emigrant
South afrikans has Retaken my Cattle which
Sinkoyella had stolen which cattle he
the said Retief now deliver unto me. —
I Dingaan King of the Zoolas as here
by Certify and declare that I thought
fit to Resign unto him the said Retief
and his Countrymen (on Reward of the
Case hereabove mentioned) the Place
Called Port Natal together with all the
Land annexed, that is to say from Dogeela
to the Omsoboebo River westward and
from the Sea to the North as far as the
Land may be Usefull and in my possession
Which I did by this and Give unto them
for their Everlasting property. —

BOTH: OLD HOUSE MUSEUM, DURBAN

Dingaan, shown above dressed for dancing, killed his half-brother to become the Zulus' chief. Later he signed a deed (left) that ceded a large portion of Zulu territory to the Dutch colonists for farming.

TEXT CONTINUED FROM PAGE 77

and prepare to meet the dangers which faced them on the other side of the mountains.

Only a few decades before the British traders and the Boer trekkers had arrived, the Zulus had become masters of Natal. Conquering their neighboring tribes by superior numbers and by well-organized ruthlessness, the Zulus had established themselves as undisputed overlords of the region. But their talent for murder and treachery was also their undoing: the chief who had led them on to so many victories was stabbed by his own half-brother. That bloody prince then became the Zulus' new ruler; his name was Dingaan.

At first Dingaan was confident enough of his own mastery to greet the newcomers in a friendly manner—the British, who had arrived by sea, and the first scouts of the Boers who were coming over the mountains. But as the

H.A.M. SWELLENGREBEL COLLECTION, BREDA, NETHERLANDS

This watercolor, painted in about 1775 by Johannes Schumacher, shows a South African community —or kraal. The natives arranged their houses in clusters and let their livestock graze in the hills.

Boers' numbers increased, so did Chief Dingaan's doubts.

Retief, for his part, was convinced that this was the land for his people. Its fertile valleys were ideal for both farming and grazing. He went to Dingaan and officially requested the grant of a large section. Dingaan's reply was somewhat reserved—he made the condition that the Boers get back for him some cattle that had been stolen by another tribe—but he agreed to give the land.

When word of the friendly agreement spread into the interior, more and more wagonloads of Boer families began to cross the mountains. And Dingaan's doubts turned to fear. On February 6, 1838, he invited Retief and about forty of his men to a celebration. As soon as everyone was within the royal enclosure, the chief rose up and shouted, "Kill the wizards!" All of the white men were murdered, and the Zulus then spread out to attack the newly founded

INFORMATION SERVICE OF SOUTH AFRICA

As British and Dutch colonists continued to pour into South Africa after Dingaan's defeat, the natives began to cling more desperately to their diminishing land. But the settlers, determined to make this rich territory theirs, called in military support to crack the natives' resistance. The painting above, done in 1852 by Thomas Baines, shows British soldiers in a pitched battle with a tribe called the Xosa. At right is a Xosa warrior posed threateningly in the path of his enemies but armed only with crude weapons that were no match for the rifles and cannon of the British.

settlements. For some months it looked as though the Zulus would triumph over the Boers as they had over the native tribes. But gradually reinforcements arrived; the newcomers to Natal began to rally. In December, 1838, the Boers, under the leadership of Andries Pretorius, launched an attack on a force of ten thousand Zulus. In a fierce battle at Blood River, Dingaan's forces were crushingly defeated. The chief himself finally perished when in 1840 he was deposed by his brother with the help of the Boers.

Though Natal was subsequently taken over by the British, the Boers had achieved their purpose of finding and developing a seacoast territory. And in the interior they held such vast regions—the Boer Republics, as they came to be called—that there was no longer any need for expansion; the Great Trek had ended.

Yet beyond the Boer Republics stretched the whole continent of Africa, with towering mountains and undiscovered lakes large enough to be called inland seas. Trekking, the peculiar form of pioneer exploration that had been sufficient to build the new nation of South Africa, did not have the force to carry north into the central and eastern regions of the continent. That force would only be supplied by individual curiosity; curiosity about the longest river in Africa—and in the world.

CAPE ARCHIVES

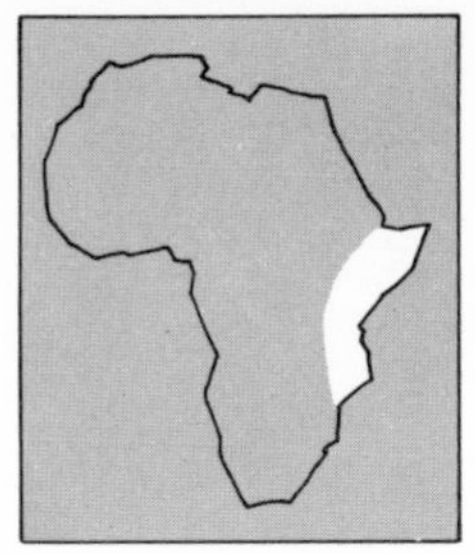

THE BRITISH IN EAST AFRICA

Late in the 1500's, Holland's monopoly on trade with the Spice Islands in the East Indies enabled her to raise the price of pepper. English merchants, afraid of being squeezed out of international commerce, sent an urgent petition to Queen Elizabeth, and in 1600 a charter was granted for an East India Company. Soon English merchant ships, like the Indiaman at right, were plowing through African, Indian, and Asian waters, their crews led by officers unrivaled for their seamanship—and their elegance (see below). When the competition for control of Africa grew in the nineteenth century, the ports where Indiamen had stopped offered Great Britain a foothold. Zanzibar, particularly, was used as a base from which to explore regions like Kenya and Uganda, which became part of British East Africa.

PERMISSION OF WILLIAM BLACKWOOD AND SONS, EDINBURGH

NATIONAL MARITIME MUSEUM, GREENWICH

SOUTH LONDON ART GALLERY, CAMBERWELL BOROUGH COUNCIL

Richard Burton's moodiness was captured in this portrait.

VI

THE VICTORIAN RIVALS

In midsummer, 1768, the Scottish explorer James Bruce arrived in Cairo and gazed out at the serene waters of the river that moved along the city's western border. The river was the Nile, and it was because of the river that Bruce had come to Africa. He intended to trace the Nile to its source, or at least to one of its sources. He would not be the last explorer to have this mission, and he was certainly not the first.

For two thousand years the north-flowing Nile had been a mystery. The ancient Egyptians had sailed and poled up the river southward from its mouth at the Mediterranean to the present city of Khartoum, where two rivers, the Blue Nile and the White Nile, come together to form the mainstream. From there on, boatmen found the river unnavigable because of the great waterfalls—or cataracts—that could easily crush the sturdiest wooden vessels. And exploration on foot was made impossible by a vast swamp called the Sudd.

Illustrated London News

Long after the Blue Nile had been explored, John Speke (above) went to Africa with Richard Burton to find the sources of the White Nile. The men became rivals and enemies.

James Bruce's goal was to find the source of the Blue Nile, which he considered the more important of the Nile's two branches. He and his party set out from Cairo and got as far upriver as Aswan, where they encountered a tribal war and were forced to make a sudden detour. They headed overland to the Red Sea and sailed south to the port of Massaua. When they turned inland again, they took a southwesterly route toward Gondar (see map on page 20).

Bruce, unlike the many men who preceded him, had a fairly accurate idea of where he was going. The source of the Blue Nile had been known centuries before; it was actually discovered in the Middle Ages by Arab traders forging into Ethiopia to look for ivory, gold, and slaves. And then in the seventeenth century a band of Portuguese missionaries saw the river's headwaters while they were exploring the mountains of Ethiopia. They observed that a trickle of water rose in the Gojjam highlands, flowed into

BIBLIOTHEQUE NATIONALE

Savages, strange beasts, and "Mountains of the Moon" (mons de la lunne) *adorn this sixteenth-century map by Le Testu*

Lake Tana, and then became the Blue Nile. But the reports these men brought back to Europe were either ignored or forgotten. By the eighteenth century the source of the river was still considered a geographic mystery.

For Bruce the problem was not so much discovery as rediscovery. He hoped to settle the issue and go on record as the man who had established the exact location of the Blue Nile's headwaters.

Bruce finally reached Gondar in February, 1770, and then traveled a few miles farther south until he found Lake Tana. Part of his work had been completed; he had only to follow the river and map its course. When at last he saw the Blue Nile flow into the White Nile, he considered his mission in Africa fulfilled.

Bruce's account of his journey and his ultimate discovery was challenged by many of his fellow explorers in Europe. And a skeptical public found his elaborate and often overblown description of native life and scenic wonders impossible to believe. His achievement was not recognized for many years, but from the time of his return from Africa the interest in solving the riddle of the Nile continued to grow.

Since ancient times, men had been fascinated by the Nile. It did not behave like an ordinary river that flooded in the rainy season and dried up in a drought. Every year, in the heat of the sweltering Egyptian summer, it rose mightily over its banks and spread across the thirsty Nile Valley. Farmers depended on it, and indeed they worshiped it. The river was the lifeblood of people who lived in the arid region around it. No wonder it was for so long a subject of curiosity and puzzlement.

Travels, Researches and Missionary Labours in South Africa, KRAPF, 1860

In this well-guarded, acorn-shaped hut, the missionary Johann Krapf was imprisoned during his search for the "Mountains of the Moon."

Writing in the second century, the geographer Ptolemy, who lived in Alexandria, asserted that the Nile flowed from two lakes fed by melting snows in a region he called the "Mountains of the Moon." No one had seen the mountains that Ptolemy designated. But no matter how hypothetical his maps may have been, they influenced explorers in Africa for hundreds of years.

Early in the eighteenth century, men began to search for the river's source by an overland route instead of defying the rapids that obstructed passage south of Egypt. Not much progress was made, however, until the mid nineteenth-century when a pair of German missionaries arrived in Africa.

Johann Ludwig Krapf and Johannes Rebmann came to the Dark Continent to preach their faith. But they quickly

SOUTH LONDON ART GALLERY, CAMBERWELL BOROUGH COUNCIL

In his journal, Burton described the town of Harar (below) as the Timbuctoo of East Africa. He was probably the first European to see it. Foreigners had been unwelcome there; he traveled to the city in Moslem disguise (right) but then presented himself as an Englishman.

First Footsteps in East Africa, BURTON, 18

caught the fever of exploration; together the two men probed the interior, mapping as they went. And the farther they went, the more intrigued they became by tales told by the natives—descriptions of giant mountains and of rich deposits of silver and gold.

From a Negro chieftain they learned of a "Country of the Moon" which lay, it was said, near some magnificent inland lakes. Might not this region be the "Mountains of the Moon" about which Ptolemy had written? Krapf and Rebmann hoped to find out. They continued their exploration into the tropical heart of East Africa, and before they turned back discovered two towering mountains covered with snow. Somewhere in that mountain area, they felt certain, lay the source of the White Nile.

But no one in Europe would listen to them. Their report received ridicule instead of praise, for who could believe that snow-capped mountains existed on the equator? It was proved later that the two Germans had discovered Mount Kilimanjaro and Mount Kenya, which are not near the source of the White Nile. The "Mountains of the Moon" (now called the Ruwenzori), which they believed they had seen, are farther west, between Uganda and the Congo. It was in this region that the headwaters of the White Nile were eventually found.

Despite the fact that Krapf and Rebmann's report of their achievements was rejected by the so-called experts of their day, England was encouraged to send an expedition to the part of East Africa that the German missionaries had mapped. England's interest in this region had increased substantially since the 1830's when the coastal areas of present-day Kenya and Tanganyika came under her influence. And the Royal Geographical Society was now convinced that the headwaters of the White Nile might be reached by land. The society favored a route originating in the east, and for a very good reason. Since the Niger had proved to have no connection with the Nile, it seemed likely that the source of the White Nile was in the east, not the west.

In 1856 the Royal Geographical Society chose two men, Richard Francis Burton and John Hanning Speke, to journey overland through East Africa to look for the headwaters of the great river. With this undertaking, a new phase of exploration began; the great age of African discovery was approaching its climax.

Although they shared a common interest in exploration in general and Africa in particular, Burton and

Speke were wholly different men. Burton was eccentric and unpredictable. Speke was methodical, and always a careful planner. The men began their African expedition as partners, although Burton was really in charge of the enterprise. But it was not long before they became bitter enemies.

Burton, who was thirty-six at the time of the expedition, had an amazing gift for languages. He had learned Arabic before he was twenty-one, while serving in the British army in India. And in order to learn more about the Indians he frequently wore Eastern clothes and often dyed his face and hands so he could mingle freely and unnoticed.

Burton had a flair for flamboyance that Speke did not share. Speke was six years younger than Burton, and by contrast was quiet and conventional. He lived up to the ideal of what a young man of the Victorian Age should be like. He rarely drank, never smoked, and seemed to be without humor, at least on the surface. He was devoted to the study of natural history, and his favorite forms of relaxation were hunting and shooting.

Speke had joined the British army in India as a seventeen-year-old cadet, and before he turned twenty-one had been struck by an urge to visit Africa. His purpose at that time had merely been to collect rare birds and animals for the natural history museum he was building in his father's home in Somerset, England. When leave was granted him, after ten years' military service, he asked permission to go to Africa and was advised to join an expedition headed by Richard Burton.

So the two men had explored in Africa for the first time in 1854. They knew the country and they had learned to get along with each other. Thus when Burton was selected to lead another expedition, whose specific purpose was to find the source of the White Nile, it was logical for him to ask Speke to accompany him. In December, 1856, the two men arrived in Zanzibar, where their expedition to the interior was to begin.

Zanzibar is a tiny island lying off the coast of modern Tanganyika. At the time of Burton and Speke's arrival, the capital city had a population of a hundred thousand and was the main depot for the slave and ivory trade to the East. Although commerce in slaves had been officially banned by the British, it was carried on illegally and at great profit. Men and women waiting to be shipped out of the country wandered through the narrow streets, naked, bewildered, often hungry and sick. As a result, cholera, smallpox, and malaria raged through the town, and dead slaves were cast away on the beaches to rot.

Zanzibar was deplorable, but it could also be beautiful. The town provided splendid comforts to those who could afford them. At times it seemed the model of a lazy tropical isle.

When he reached Zanzibar, Burton immediately began arranging for a caravan to the interior. His expedition, when finally organized, was composed of more than a hundred carriers, servants, and guards. In addition, he enlisted about twenty soldiers from the sultan of Zanzibar and hired two personal servants who would act as cooks.

Among the supplies brought along on the expedition were some of the latest European weapons and scientific instruments plus tents, camp beds, tables, chairs, air pillows, and a small library. There were also carpenters' and blacksmiths' tools, and a portable boat. For himself and his young associate, Burton took along a dozen bottles of brandy, a box of cigars, thirty pounds of tea, and a medicine chest that contained a good supply of quinine. This

PEABODY MUSEUM, SALEM

Zanzibar, the gateway to East Africa, attracted trade from all parts of the world. An American vessel (left) lies at anchor in the fine, wide harbor.

In the engraving above, Burton (at center) seems more like an uncouth prospector than the cultured, multilingual man of many disguises that he was. The engraving shows Burton and his party plodding through East Africa. They can be seen at right paddling across Lake Tanganyika. Both pictures are from the first edition of Burton's journal.

medicine had been used for some time to fight malaria, but unfortunately Burton did not have much faith in it.

The men moved their supplies and the carriers they had been able to hire in Zanzibar to the mainland. Here at the village of Bagamoyo they discovered that only thirty-six more porters were available. It became necessary to buy a number of donkeys—at prices much higher than the cost of buying men—and to leave much of the heavier baggage behind, including the portable boat. Finally, the caravan set out on June 25, 1857.

The coastal plain of East Africa can be hot and unpleasant, but about a hundred miles inland, the terrain rises to a wind-swept plateau. This tableland, which averages about three thousand feet in height, extends across East and Central Africa to the western Congo. Thus the part of the continent that follows the equator is less a land of steaming jungles than one of rolling hills and high plateaus. Once they had reached the plateau country, Burton and Speke realized that the presence of tall mountains, as reported by Krapf and Rebmann, was certainly not improbable.

The expedition was soon able to recruit more carriers, and finally it numbered 132 persons. They were now head-

ing toward Kazeh, an Arab trading post situated two thirds of the way between the Indian Ocean and Lake Tanganyika. This town, today called Tabora, is the modern junction of railroad lines from the lake country of the north and west. The caravan arrived there in November, 1857, after a five months' journey. The men had averaged about a hundred miles a month; their trip so far had been quite comfortable, under the circumstances.

Burton was overjoyed to see the Arabs in Kazeh. Because he spoke Arabic fluently he felt that he was again among friends. Moreover, he had developed an intense dislike of the Negroes—a feeling that Speke never shared or condoned. This difference in attitude caused considerable friction between the two men. They were growing cooler to each other, and from this point on Burton's journal rarely mentions Speke except to ridicule him.

The fact is that they had not been the best of friends when the expedition began. Their relationship had been scarred by the disastrous ending of their first African adventure when they were attacked by some fierce Somali tribesmen. During the encounter Speke ran back to the

BOTH: *The Lake Regions of Central Africa*, BURTON, 1860

protection of his tent. He did this, he said later, so he could get a clearer view of his attackers, but Burton misunderstood his movements. Burton called out, "Don't step back or they will think we are retiring!"

Speke could only assume that this was meant as a comment on his courage. He was wounded in this encounter and then captured and tortured. But long after the wounds had healed and the pain had been forgotten, Burton's words continued to rankle. This incident in itself did not bring about a breach between the two men, but the hatred they later felt for each other could probably be traced back to it.

Early in December, 1857, Burton and Speke headed west from Kazeh, and the following February discovered

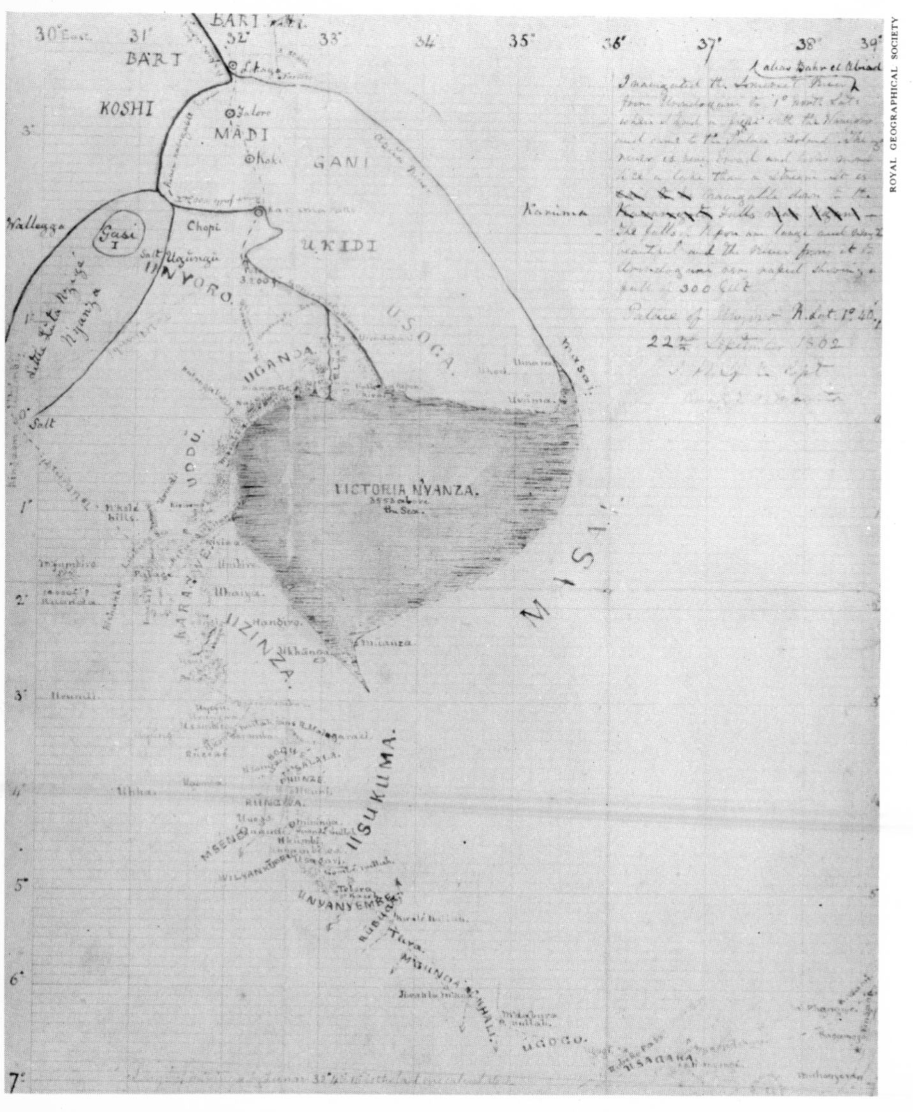

This is a portion of the map Speke sketched after making a journey to Lake Victoria. The lake is called Victoria N'yanza on the drawing.

ROYAL GEOGRAPHICAL SOCIETY

Lake Tanganyika. On the shores of the lake was an Arab trading post called Ujiji, which had been established barely a dozen years before.

Burton and Speke's discovery of Lake Tanganyika was a major event. Whatever else happened, their expedition could now be considered a success, but both men were seriously ill. Burton had suffered from continual bouts with malaria since leaving Kazeh, and now he was afflicted with a painful abscess that had developed in his jaw. Speke had become nearly blind from the sudden worsening of an eye disease that had troubled him since his childhood. Thus he described the expedition's first view of the lake rather dryly: "From the summit of the eastern horn, the lovely Tanganyika Lake could be seen in all its glory by everyone but myself."

When Speke's eyesight at last improved, the two men made a hurried exploration of the lake, which Burton believed was the source of the White Nile. This began to seem unlikely, however, for their instruments indicated that the lake was only ten feet higher than the known level of the White Nile at Gondokoro, almost six hundred miles to the north. Burton knew that the descent of any river must be steeper than that if it is hold to its banks, but he was not yet willing to concede defeat. He wanted to investigate further, but his illness had so weakened him that he had to return to Ujiji.

SOUTH LONDON ART GALLERY, CAMBERWELL BOROUGH COUNCIL

Flamboyant Richard Burton holds a native spear in this rare photograph that was taken in his tent.

In June, 1858, the caravan arrived in Kazeh. Burton was much in need of rest and eager to complete his notes on the progress of the trip. Thus when an Arab trader described another lake—this one bigger and perhaps at a higher altitude than Tanganyika—Speke requested permission to go off and see it himself. Burton let him go, possibly with some relief, and the younger man took one gun carrier and a small party of porters and guards with him.

In exactly twenty-five days Speke reached the great lake which the natives called Ukerewe and which he christened Victoria after England's reigning queen. He was convinced, the moment he saw the lake, that it was the long-sought source of the White Nile. Later he wrote: "The caravan . . . began winding up a long but gradually inclined hill—which, as it bears no name, I shall call Somerset—until it reached its summit, when the vast expanse of the pale blue waters of the [lake] burst suddenly on my gaze. It was early morning. The distant sea line of the north horizon was defined in the calm atmosphere between the north and west points of the compass . . . I no longer felt any doubt that the lake at my feet gave birth to that interesting river, the source of which has been the subject of so much speculation, and the object of so many explorers."

Speke hurried back to Kazeh to inform the ailing Burton of his discovery. The older man was unimpressed by his assistant's assertion that he had found the source of the White Nile. As usual Burton ridiculed him and succeeded in making Speke more adamant. They argued bitterly.

Speke was substantially right, and his chief was wrong (as illustrated by the charts opposite), but Burton's contention was not motivated entirely by jealousy. As Speke had seen but a small portion of the lake's south shore, his convictions could be based only on supposition. He had merely had an "inspiration," as Burton pointedly reminded him, and that was by no means conclusive proof.

Neither man would back down, and the argument was finally abandoned. In September of that year the two explorers loaded their caravan and began the long return trip to the coast. By this time both men were desperately ill—Burton with malaria and Speke with pneumonia and pleurisy. They were so weak they had to be carried, and the caravan did not reach the African coast until February, 1859. From there they made their way to Aden, a settlement on the southwest coast of Arabia.

Burton remained in Aden in an attempt to recuperate, while Speke immediately booked passage to England. They agreed that nothing should be published about their exploration unless they both could take credit for it. And before he embarked, Speke gave Burton his word that he would disclose nothing about the expedition until Burton himself had arrived in London.

Speke did not keep his promise, however. The strength of his conviction apparently got the better of him, and when he arrived in London he went straight to the Royal Geographical Society and made the claim that he had discovered the source of the White Nile. Moreover, the society accepted his findings and later asked him to return to Africa at the head of his own expedition.

When Richard Burton at last landed in England, still weak from illness, he found himself almost completely forgotten. His report on Lake Tanganyika as the true source of the White Nile was received coolly and without much interest. Wrong or right, he was treated badly, and he never forgave his former subordinate, John Speke, as long as the young man lived.

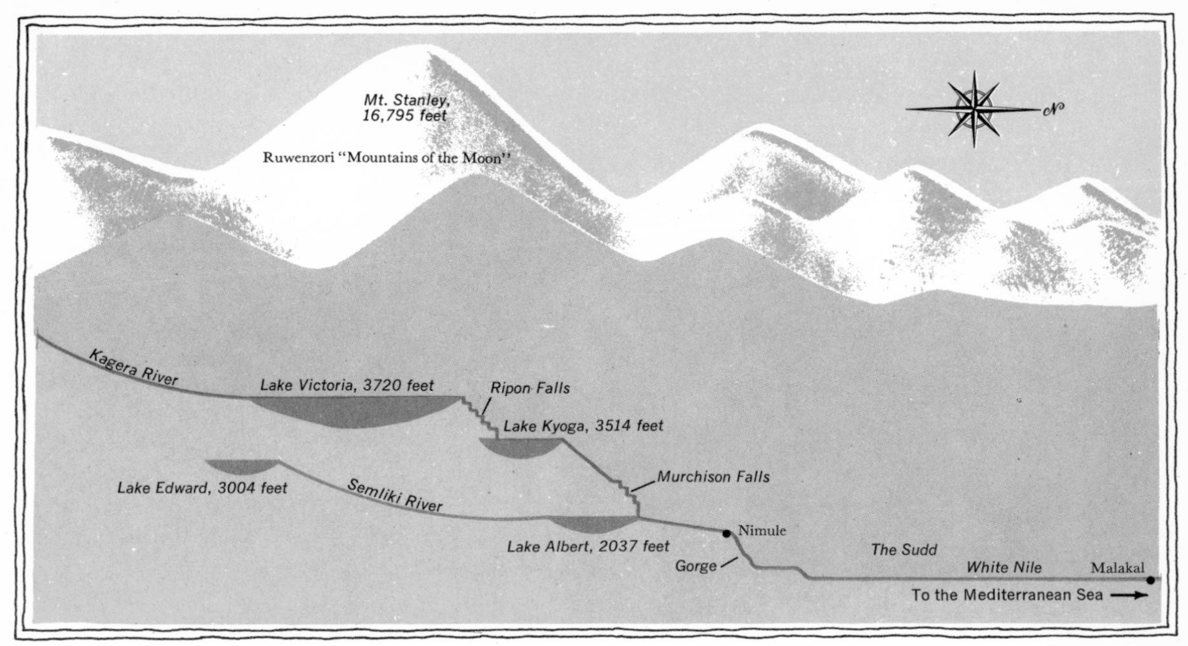

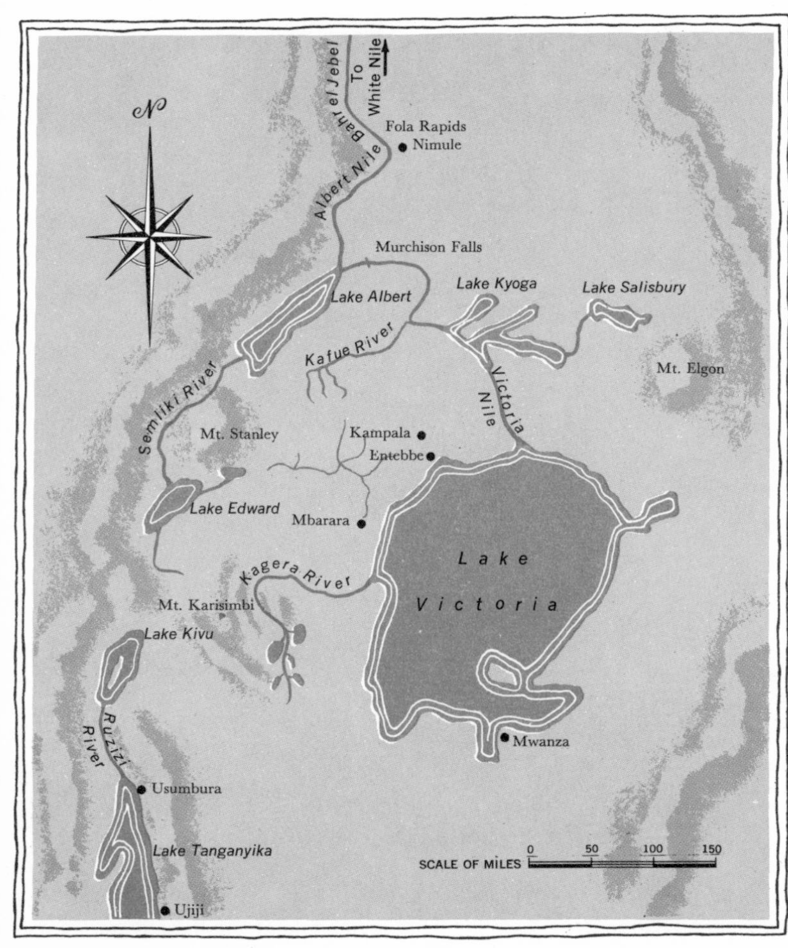

HEADWATERS OF THE WHITE NILE

Long concealed in the valleys of mountainous Uganda, the origins of the White Nile are still difficult to locate—even with the aid of a modern map (left). The river rises in mountain streams flowing into Lake Victoria and winds along rocky channels and over wide rapids until it pours into Lake Albert. Then passing through a swamplike valley, it reaches the Sudd—where thick, floating vegetation makes it unnavigable except for small craft. Farther north, near Khartoum, the Blue Nile joins the White Nile and they continue as one river through the desert. In the chart above, real distances have been distorted so the gradual descent of the river can be seen. From the "Mountains of the Moon" to the Mediterranean, the Nile River drops six thousand feet.

VII

FOUNTAINS OF THE NILE

James Grant was Speke's old friend, who had hunted with him in India.

The man Speke chose to accompany him on his return trip to Lake Victoria proved a perfect second-in-command. James Augustus Grant was the same age as Speke, trustworthy, and submissive as well—qualities of character that Speke himself had not displayed when he served under Burton. As Grant wrote in his book, *A Walk Across Africa*, "Not a shade of jealousy or distrust or even ill temper ever came between us." As these were precisely the feelings that had come between Burton and Speke, the virtue in this particular case must have been wholly Grant's.

The two men set out from Zanzibar with a large caravan in September, 1860. It took them more than a year to reach the unknown plateau country west of Lake Tanganyika. In that high heartland of Central Africa, Speke and Grant came upon three native kingdoms that made up part of the present country of Uganda. For centuries people who lived to the west and north of the lake had been building a civilization that was almost completely cut off from the outside world. Karagwe in the south was the weakest of their three states. Buganda and Bunyoro in the north were the strongest and were bitter rivals.

The travelers remained awhile in Karagwe, where the king treated them cordially. Then early in 1862 they headed north—all except Grant, who had a painful leg sore that made walking impossible.

In Buganda, Speke insisted on being treated as a visiting noble instead of as a trader. He was granted an audience with the king, but the explorer fumed at being made to wait in the hot sun until the king was ready to receive him. After a few minutes' pause Speke turned on his heel and returned to camp.

After leaving Lake Victoria, the upper Nile flows serenely until it reaches Murchison Falls (right) where its waters plunge 130 feet into a misty gorge.

The Albert N'Yanza, BAKER, 1866

The king's courtiers were dumbfounded, for no visitor had ever behaved so imperiously. They ran after Speke and urged him to return with them to the palace, assuring him that their leader would see him right away. They even gave him permission to bring a chair to sit on during the interview. This was unprecedented, for no man but the chief was ever allowed to sit on anything but earth.

When he arrived at the royal court, Speke presented the native king with a number of gifts, including, pointedly, an iron chair, as well as several carbines and a revolver. In the book he later wrote, Speke described the king as "a good-looking, well-figured, tall young man of twenty-five" whom he found "sitting on a red blanket spread upon a square platform of royal grass encased in tiger reeds . . ."

For an hour the two men, native king and English explorer, sat and stared at each other without exchanging a word. Then when it was growing dark, a messenger approached the explorer to ask if he had seen the king. "Yes, for one full hour," Speke replied rather testily. When this reply was translated for the king, he rose to his feet, took his spear in hand, and silently left the enclosure. He walked on his toes in imitation, it was said, of a lion.

Speke was stunned. Had he been insulted? No, not at all, he was assured. Actually, he had been treated very courteously, for the king, who was now eating dinner, had delayed having his meal until Speke arrived for the interview.

Speke continued to be treated respectfully throughout his stay, perhaps because he had established his right to royal privilege. After Speke had spent three months in Buganda, Grant arrived, his condition improved despite a lingering limp. The men made plans to leave Buganda, but the king was not eager to let them go. He enjoyed the presence of white men in his court. Besides, he was convinced that the longer they stayed the more gifts he could get them to give him. He delayed their departure for six more weeks; finally, on July 7, 1862, he allowed them to depart.

The men headed north toward a river they believed to be the first stage of the White Nile. This river, now called the Victoria Nile, runs northwest between Lake Victoria and a body of water that was discovered two years later and

Journal of the Discovery of the Source of the Nile, SPEKE, 1864

This engraving from Speke's journal shows him introducing Grant (left) to Buganda's dowager queen, whom he described as "fair, fat, and forty-five," and only rarely sober.

Artist J. W. Wilson created an African setting for John Speke's portrait. A rifle and a sextant are beside the explorer; Lake Victoria is behind him.

BRITISH INFORMATION SERVICE

Africa's Kamba people still cling to ancient customs, one of which is the frenzied dancing that is traditionally performed on feast days.

named Lake Albert. Speke followed this river alone for some time, having sent Grant to open up the way to Bunyoro, the third native kingdom in the region. On July 28 Speke came to a series of rapids. They were only thirteen feet high but very broad, and from the volume of water that poured over them Speke was certain he had seen the first outpouring of a great river.

In his book, Speke described the rapids as "a sight that attracted one to it for hours—the roar of the waters, the thousands of passenger fish leaping at the falls with all their might . . . hippopotami and crocodiles lying sleepily on the water . . . and cattle driven down to drink."

He named these rapids Ripon Falls, after Lord Ripon, the man who had presided over the Royal Geographical Society at the time Speke's expedition was organized. Now the explorer was certain he had reached his goal and that his work was done. He was not certain, however, that he and Grant could stay alive long enough to find their way out again to tell the news. Their supplies were dangerously low, and they were both exhausted.

Cutting across country as quickly as he could, Speke rejoined Grant, and together the two men and their caravan—now vastly reduced because of disease and desertion—marched into Bunyoro. King Kamrasi, who ruled this land, was a moody and suspicious man, and a greedy one too. He robbed them of much of their remaining supplies before they could get away. At last they moved northward again. Their only hope, they thought, was to meet a relief expedition that was supposed to reach them with fresh supplies and additional carriers. The explorers were a year late for the rendezvous, and they were afraid they might have been given up for lost.

But the slim hope of rescue drove them on. They tramped through jungle and scrubland and across vast stretches of grassland. And whenever they could they floated downstream on the Nile. All around them were hostile tribes of painted natives, fiercer and more primitive than any they had encountered before. One time these natives attacked the caravan, in Speke's words, "dancing like so many devils, with sheaves of burning grass in their hands."

On February 15, 1863, Speke and Grant stumbled into the upper Nile trading station of Gondokoro. There, to their surprise and joy, they were met by a hearty Englishman named Samuel Baker. He and his wife had come up the Nile hoping to find them.

"What joy this was I can hardly tell," wrote Speke, who had known Baker many years before. "We could not talk fast enough, so overwhelmed were we both to meet again." Soon Speke and Grant also encountered the official relief expedition that had come to rescue them, and then sailed down the Nile to Cairo. When they finally returned to London more than two and a half years after they had left, they were greeted warmly by the Royal Geographical Society, which had sent them, and by a public that had waited for them anxiously.

Meanwhile, the Bakers continued their journey, taking up the task of Nile exploration themselves. To almost anyone but Samuel Baker the thought of bringing a woman into the wilds of an uncharted country would have seemed foolhardy—particularly when the odds against survival were so great. But Baker was a most uncommon man, and his wife was a remarkable woman. Their undertaking proved every bit as hazardous as that of Burton, Speke, and Grant, and the Bakers acquitted themselves brilliantly.

They had arrived in Africa in 1861 while Speke and Grant were still plodding through Tanganyika. Since Baker and his wife were under no instructions from any scientific or religious society, they could do exactly as they pleased. They hoped to meet Speke and Grant on the way up the

Heroes of the Dark Continent, BUELL, 1890

Sir Samuel Baker, MURRAY AND WHITE, 1895

This picture of Samuel Baker, from a biography published in 1895, was drawn after the Egyptians made him a pasha ("lord of the empire").

Boatloads of screaming savages harassed the Bakers during their trip through Africa's lake country.

Nile, but they had other plans as well. After spending fourteen months exploring the tributaries that flowed from Ethiopia into the great river, they went to Khartoum in June, 1862, and prepared for a journey up the White Nile.

Khartoum, at the time the Bakers went there, had been in existence only forty years. Like Zanzibar, it was used chiefly as a trading post for exchanging slaves and ivory. Mr. and Mrs. Baker detested the place and decided to leave it as quickly as they could. They were delayed, however, for it took them six months to acquire three ships and a hundred men to take them up the Nile to Gondokoro.

The traders in Khartoum, afraid the Bakers would try to prevent the capture of slaves, did not want the couple to go farther south. The town's Egyptian governor even sent an official to halt the expedition. But when Baker threatened to toss him overboard, the official readily backed down. As it happened, Samuel Baker had no great love for the Negroes. He probably did not condone the cruelty of the slave merchants, but he did not outwardly favor the abolition of slavery.

The Bakers and their flotilla left for Gondokoro in December, 1862. When they arrived, they deposited all their stores with an Egyptian merchant. He was instructed to deliver half of these supplies to Speke and Grant if they should happen to arrive while the couple was off exploring the interior.

These instructions proved needless, for thirteen days after the Bakers came to Gondokoro, Speke and Grant—and the remnants of their weary caravan—pulled into town. Considering the delays endured by each party, the timing of this meeting seems incredible. The Bakers were not particularly surprised to see the two Englishmen despite the odd coincidence, but they could not help feeling a sense of disappointment that they had not shared in the discovery of the source of the White Nile. Baker even said to Speke, with characteristic candor, "Does not one leaf of the laurel remain for me?" Speke replied by assuring Baker that there was, in fact, a whole branch of laurel left to pick.

As Baker later wrote: "[Speke] gave me a map of their route showing that they had been unable to complete the actual exploration of the Nile, and that a most important portion still remained to be determined . . . I now heard that the field was not only open but that additional interest was given to the exploration by the proof that the Nile flowed out of one great lake, the Victoria, but that it evidently must derive an additional supply from an unknown lake as it entered [this lake] at the northern extremity."

Immediately they decided they would have to see this "unknown lake." The Bakers had seen Speke's map and knew where they were going, but the way was not without hardship and peril. They set out in March, 1863, and by the end of the year they had to buy and train three oxen to replace their exhausted horses.

Soon Baker began to suffer from attacks of fever. He had brought along quinine, and he and his wife had used it faithfully, but as they had been away from Gondokoro for ten months, their supply was exhausted. In the beginning, Mrs. Baker suffered from disease far less than her husband and generally bore up admirably under the strain of travel. She was never frightened by the thumping of war drums or the sight of savages dancing. And if she heard the stealthy tread of an intruder sneaking into camp at night, she would awaken her husband calmly. "She was not a *screamer*," he wrote of her, which summed up her character and at the same time praised it succinctly.

Near the end of January the Bakers managed to get themselves ferried across the Victoria Nile, and on February 10, 1864, reached Bunyoro. King Kamrasi was as surly to them as he had been to Speke and Grant. And he extorted from them almost everything they possessed. The couple was nearly helpless, for by now fever gripped them both. Defying illness and exhaustion, they pushed on toward the lake, which was only a few weeks' march away.

The Albert N'Yanza. BAKER. 1866

King Kamrasi tried to delay the Bakers in the hope of receiving more gifts from them. Finally, in February, 1864, Samuel Baker mounted his ox and set out leading his expedition; a rifle persuaded the king's men to let him pass.

The Masai were once the fiercest tribe in all East Africa. Deadly weapons were made for their use: the clubs at the bottom of this assemblage and the longest spears. The short spears with flat, spade-shaped tips were for boy warriors. The pouchlike object shown here is in reality a headdress that was worn as a hood. There is also an arm band made of ivory, a horseshoe-shaped collar, and furry anklets for dancers.

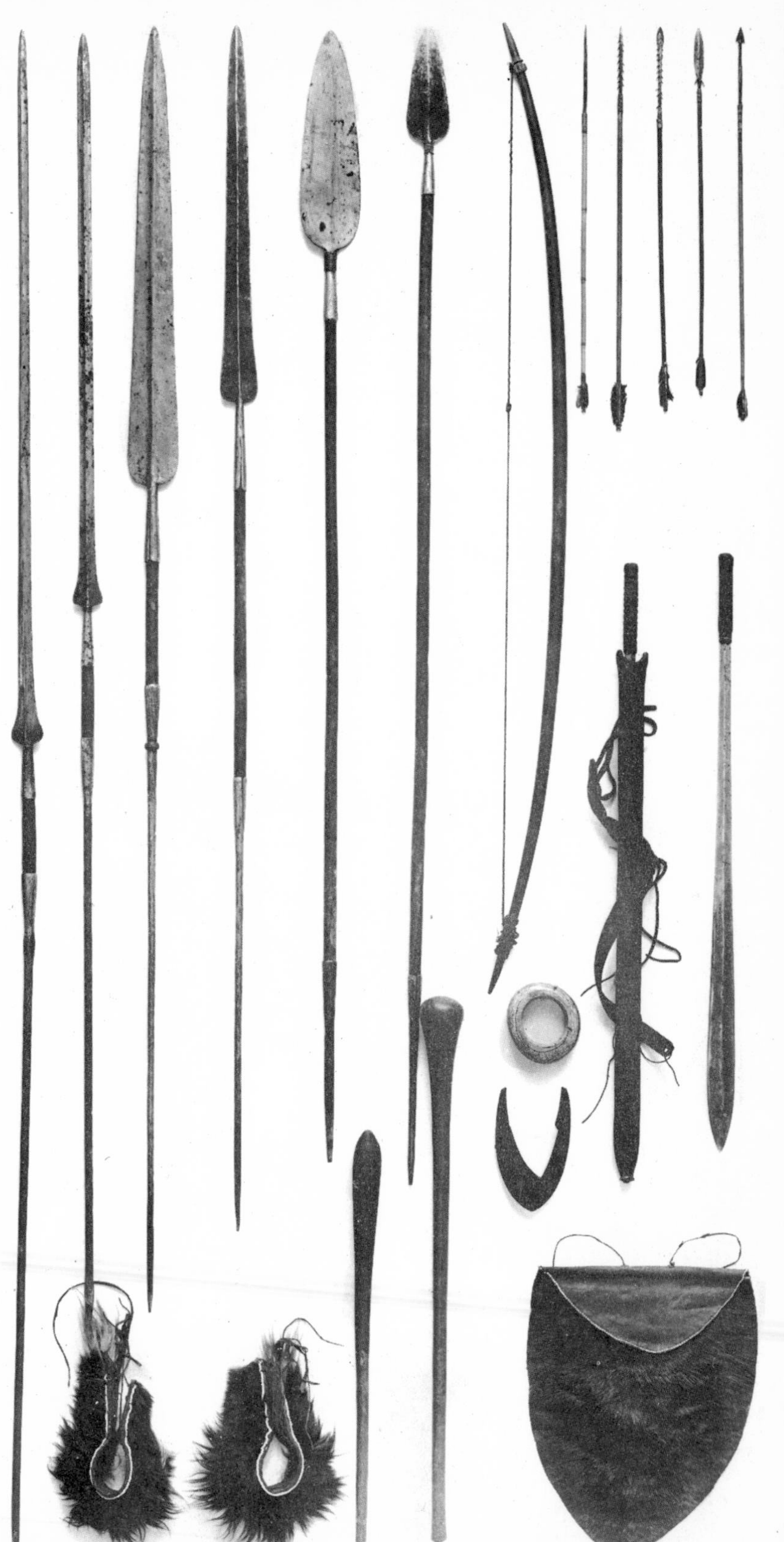

Before long, Mrs. Baker grew too weak to do much walking; there were times when she had to be carried on a litter fashioned from wicker bedsteads. At one point, when a swampy river barred the way, the caravan crossed carefully on a natural bridge composed of piled-up vegetation. Here is how Baker described the crossing: "I led the way, and begged Mrs. Baker to follow me on foot as quickly as possible, precisely in my tracks. The river was about eighty yards wide, and I had scarcely completed a fourth of the distance and looked back to see if my wife followed close to me when I was horrified to see her standing in one spot and sinking gradually through the weeds, while her face was distorted and perfectly purple."

The explorer rushed back and managed to rescue her. "I dragged her," he wrote, "like a corpse through the yielding vegetation, and up to our waists we scrambled across to the other side, just keeping her head above water." When they reached the opposite bank, Baker realized that his wife was suffering from sunstroke.

As there was no food here, the caravan pressed on two

The design painted on each shield at right indicates the age of the Masai who used it, and the clan he belonged to. During some of the Masai rituals, pompons were put on lances as a sign of peace.

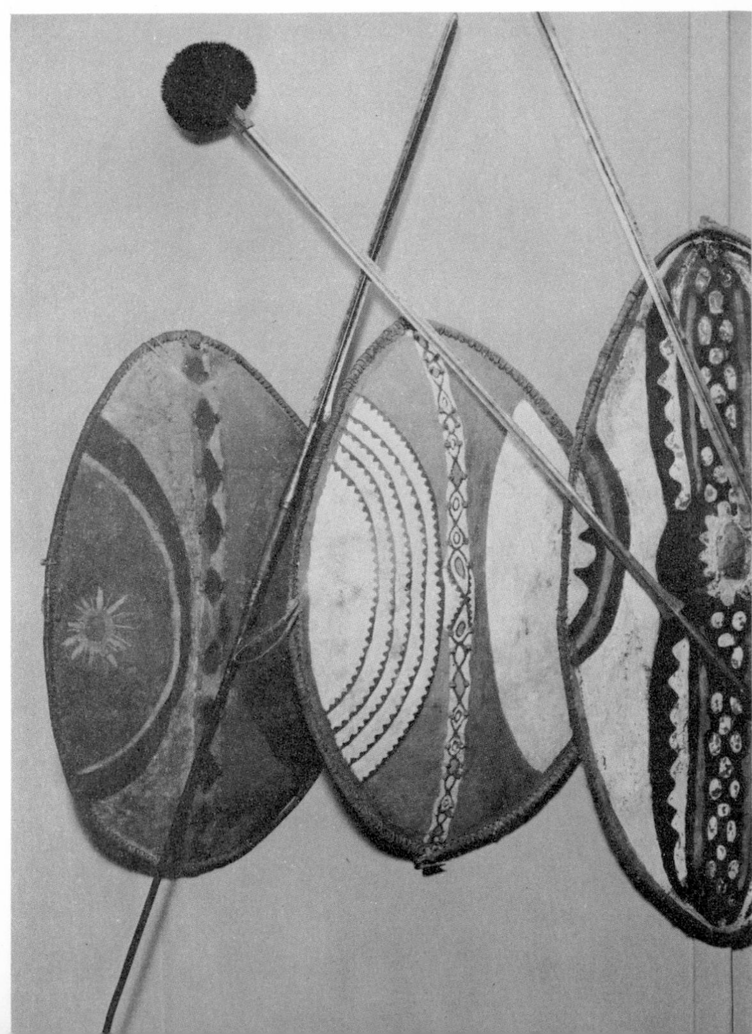

more days, and porters carried the unconscious woman. Baker kept watch over her for two days—until on the third morning she awoke delirious. It was raining now as Baker and his carriers continued their march, searching desperately for food. As Baker later recalled, "For seven days I had not slept, and although as weak as a reed, I had marched by the side of her litter. Nature could resist no longer. We reached a village one evening; she had been in violent convulsions successively—it was all but over. I laid her down on her litter within a hut; covered her with a Scotch plaid; and I fell upon my mat insensible, worn out with sorrow and fatigue. My men put a new handle to the pickaxe that evening, and sought for a dry spot to dig her grave." But Florence Baker was not to be counted out yet. When her husband awoke after his own collapse, he found her calm and well again; after two days' convalescence she was ready to resume the journey.

At daybreak on March 14, 1864, the caravan reached the summit of a low hill. And there, as Baker reported, "the glory of our prize burst suddenly before me! There, like a sea of quicksilver, lay . . . the grand expanse of water—a boundless sea-horizon on the south and southwest, glittering in the noonday sun . . ." There was a zigzag path down to the water, but this was so steep that the oxen they were riding could not negotiate it. But the Bakers could—and did. Supported by a stick of stout bamboo and "strengthened by success," they tottered down the cliff and walked through sandy meadows to the water's edge.

"The waves were rolling upon a white pebbly beach," Baker recalled. "I rushed into the lake, and thirsty with heat and fatigue, with a heart full of gratitude, I drank deeply from the sources of the Nile." And then, as "an imperishable memorial of one loved and mourned by our gracious queen . . . I called this great lake the Albert . . . The Victoria and Albert lakes are the two sources of the Nile."

The Bakers had reached their objective and enjoyed their moment of triumph. Now they had to get back. They obtained crude canoes from some native fishermen and proceeded north along the shores of Lake Albert. They finally reached the point where the Victoria Nile enters the lake. Sailing upstream they came upon a magnificent waterfall. Baker named it Murchison Falls after Sir Roderick Murchison, who had become president of the Royal Geographical Society.

The return trip overland proved as perilous as the

Queen Victoria and Prince Albert set the tone of an age known for its love of sport, gentility, and animals. Sir Edwin Landseer did this painting of the royal family.

first leg of the journey. But who could doubt that the Bakers would get through? When they reached England at last, Samuel Baker was knighted, and Florence Baker, now Lady Baker, very promptly became the rage of London society. Loyally, and in all sincerity, Baker gave credit to "the devoted companion of my pilgrimage, to whom I owed success and life—my wife."

Before they arrived in England, however, the Bakers were shocked and aggrieved to learn of the death of the man who had made their success possible, John Hanning Speke. They also learned that though Speke and Grant had been widely acclaimed upon returning to England, there was still some doubt as to the measure of the men's achievement. After all, it was said, Speke had not followed the entire course of the river that flowed out of Lake Victoria. Therefore, it was not inconceivable that the Nile might have yet another source. Richard Burton was one of the strongest proponents of this argument, and soon a full-blown controversy raged.

At last it was decided that Burton and Speke should confront each other at a public meeting. The younger man dreaded the encounter, probably because he knew how persuasive Burton could be. At any rate, the encounter was never held. While Burton was on the platform and the audience had been kept waiting twenty-five minutes, word came that Speke had been killed in a hunting accident. There was some polite Victorian speculation at the time that Speke's death had really been suicide, and for a while it seemed that Burton had won his point—and had been avenged.

This victory, however sweet, was not long-lasting. The report that the Bakers brought back to England the following year tended to substantiate Speke's findings. But still there were many people who doubted his theories, and to a certain extent their doubts may have been justified. It had been proved that the Victoria Nile ran from Lake Victoria to Lake Albert. It had also been shown that a river issued toward the north from Lake Albert and that this river was probably the White Nile. But what about Lake Albert itself? Baker had not explored the entire circumference of the lake; thus if there should prove to be a river entering the lake at its southern end, that river might have to be considered the true source of the Nile. A glance at the map on page 101 will indicate that this was by no means an outlandish idea. Lake Edward lies just south of Lake Albert, and south of that is Lake Kivu, which is in turn connected to Lake Tanganyika by the Ruzizi River. If all these lakes had actually been joined, then Lake Tanganyika would be the true source of the Nile, just as Burton had insisted.

Since the question was still unsettled, the Royal Geographical Society decided to send out one other man to try and solve the mystery. This man, who was destined to become the greatest explorer of his time, was David Livingstone.

Shaped like a gnarled root on this vivid seventeenth-century Arab map, the Nile winds through palm-studded oases on its way north (bottom) to the sea.

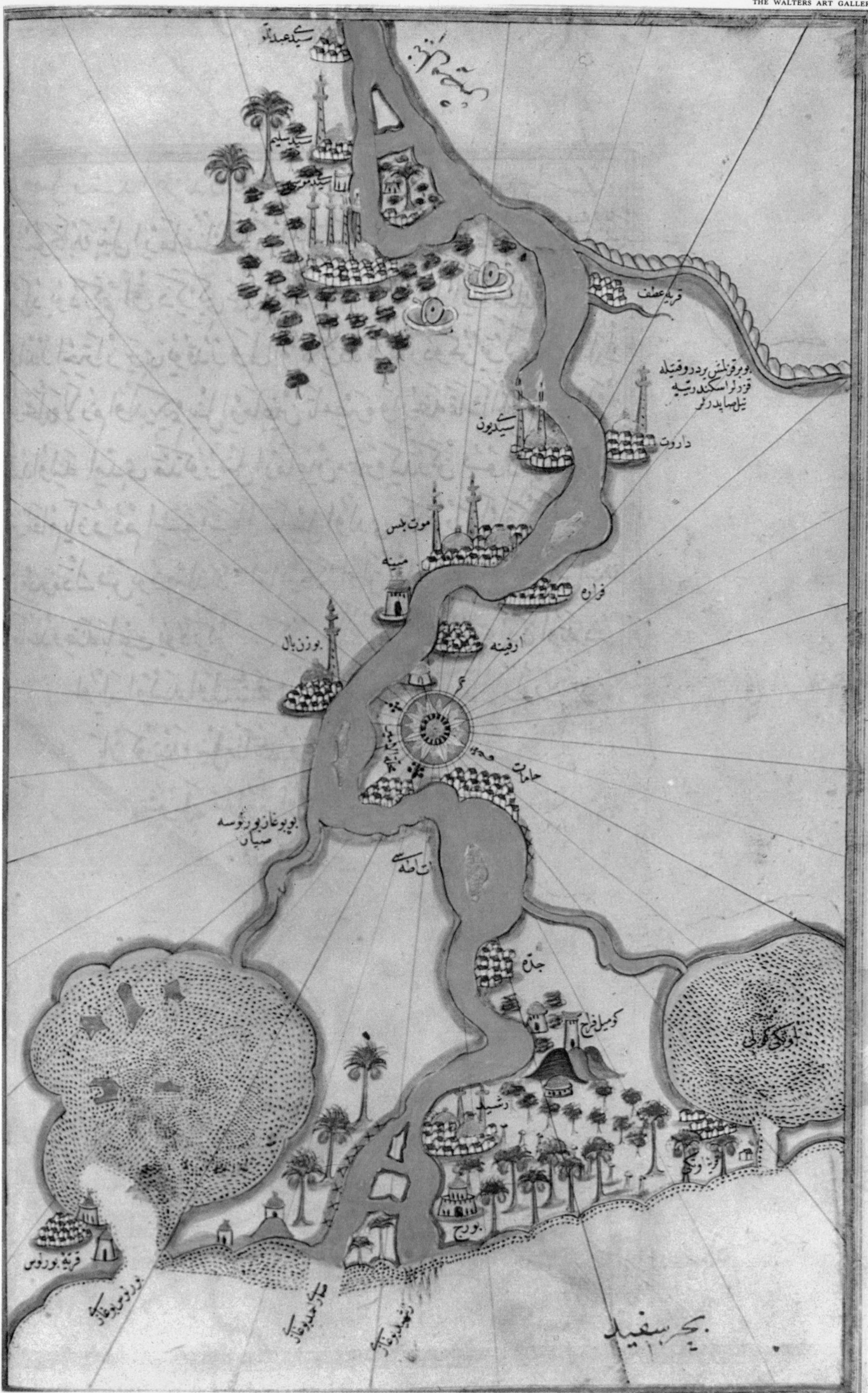

بحر سفید

VIII

DR. LIVINGSTONE

David Livingstone was born at Blantyre, Scotland, on March 23, 1813. When he was ten he went to work in a cotton mill, and with his first wages began to buy books which he managed to read while working at his spinning machine. Later he used his summer earnings as a spinner to send himself to nearby Glasgow in the winter to study medicine and theology. Then in 1840 he sailed for Cape Town to become a medical missionary in Africa.

Unlike such men as Samuel Baker and Richard Burton, Livingstone had a high regard for the African Negroes—perhaps because he understood their way of life better and was more sympathetic to their unhappy station. He was shocked by what he saw of the African slave trade, which still flourished in the 1840's, even though it had been officially outlawed.

Slave merchants had been among the very first explorers in Africa. Their arrival in a new territory resembled an invasion, for they raided villages and burned homes in cruel assaults. Their objective was to capture the hardiest specimens and drag them aboard the jam-packed slave ships. The slave trade expanded as the demand for slaves increased in Mediterranean countries and in the East. And because so many Negroes themselves contributed to the flow of slave traffic, any attempt to abolish slavery seemed futile. Native chieftains had turned into smalltime tycoons, trading their tribesmen for trinkets, and the work of the slavers was becoming not only less difficult but more profitable.

The antislavery interests concluded that the best way to end slavery would be to encourage other forms of trade among the natives. They were certain that slavery could

Livingstone, who spent much of his life in the wilds of Africa, looks like a sedate scholar in Frederick Havill's portrait, painted from a photograph.

NATIONAL PORTRAIT GALLERY, LONDON

Heroes of the Dark Continent, BUELL, 1890

Poling their small boat through a forest of reeds in the upper Shire River, Livingstone and his native bearers found Lake Nyasa in 1859.

not continue if the African continent were opened up fully to commerce and colonization. This was called the positive policy for achieving abolition, and young David Livingstone was soon one of its greatest exponents.

His first station in Africa was at Kuruman, about 120 miles northwest of Kimberley on the southern edge of the Kalahari Desert. There he set about visiting neighboring settlements and learning the native Bechuana language. Dr. Robert Moffat was chief of the mission station, and in 1844 Livingstone married Moffat's oldest daughter, Mary. During the next few years Livingstone and his wife built several more mission stations, but by this time the young doctor was becoming more and more eager to strike deeper into the interior. He had heard that a "land of waters and forests" existed beyond Lake Ngami at the far side of the Kalahari Desert, and his curiosity had been aroused.

The opportunity for him to explore this unknown region presented itself in 1849 when two wealthy game hunters, William C. Oswell and Mungo Murray, came to Africa. They invited Livingstone to act as interpreter and accompany their hunting party on an expedition north across the desert. Two months later they reached Lake Ngami in the western part of what is now Bechuanaland. They were probably the first white men to see that region. Compared to what Livingstone later accomplished, however, this was no great feat of exploration, but it did excite considerable interest back in England. In 1851 the doctor traveled north again with Oswell, and at Sesheke discovered the rushing waters of the upper Zambezi River.

Peering across the river that wound through woodland and meadow, Livingstone could not help wondering where it went. Did it connect with the Congo? Did it flow into one of the rivers at the source of the Nile? Livingstone was determined to find out, but floods and malaria kept him from following the river then.

ROYAL GEOGRAPHICAL SOCIETY

A native once said that the sextant (above) gave Livingstone the power to "take the sun down from the heavens and place it under his arm."

Yet he remained convinced of the commercial importance of his discovery of the Zambezi. As he wrote in a letter to his parents, the slave trade had only recently come to the region around Sesheke, which was occupied by a people known as the Makololo. He had extracted a promise from the Makololo not to barter in slaves, but Livingstone believed that "the only effectual means of putting a stop to the trade would be to supply the market with English goods in exchange for the products of their country." And what better avenue for this trade than the Zambezi itself?

"I feel assured," wrote Livingstone, "that if Christian merchants would establish a legitimate commerce on the Zambezi they would drive slave dealers out of the market, and would certainly be no losers in the end." Initially, at least, his desire to explore the Zambezi was prompted by a passionate belief that if he succeeded in marking out trade routes in southern Africa, the institution of slavery would topple.

In April, 1852, he returned to Cape Town with his

ROYAL GEOGRAPHICAL SOCIETY

wife and children, whom he then sent back to England. Next he set about collecting supplies for another expedition to the north. The Boers at the Cape were unfriendly, however. Because they wanted no interference with slavery, they spread reports that Livingstone had sold arms to the natives and had tried to incite a rebellion. A short time later, in fact, some Boers attacked Livingstone's last mission station at Kolobeng and destroyed all his belongings. It was a vicious act, but they felt justified in doing it, for they continued to be suspicious and distrustful of the doctor.

By the following year Livingstone had penetrated deep into the country east of Lake Ngami. At last in May, 1853, he came to Linyanti, the Makololo capital, where he was welcomed by the chief of the tribe. Livingstone's plan was to sail upstream on the Zambezi and eventually strike out westward across the continent to the port city of Loanda

A portion of Baines' painting of the Ma-Robert *passing an angry bull elephant is on the cover of this book. The artist, accompanying Livingstone, was aboard the ship.*

(now Luanda) on the west coast of Portuguese Angola.

A party of Makololo agreed to accompany him, and they made the journey by boat and by land. It was Livingstone's custom to travel light, for his needs were few. At first the party advanced without undue hardships. But by early 1854, the food supply was short, and when the rainy season came, the entire party found itself sloshing uncomfortably across meadows that were ankle deep in water. Malaria and dysentery were rampant, and at one point the men, weary of the miserable journey, threatened to mutiny. Recalling the grim occasion, Livingstone wrote, "Knowing that our lives depended on vigorously upholding authority, I seized a double-barreled pistol and darted out looking, I suppose, so savage as to put them to flight." He never had trouble with his men again.

By April, 1854, the expedition had arrived at Cassange, which was a relatively large Portuguese trading station. The first European Livingstone met there asked to see his passport and then explained that the explorer would have to be taken to the authorities. Livingstone was delighted to go, for as he explained, he was "very much in the position of people who commit a minor offense if only to obtain board and lodging in prison." However, the commandant of the station fed him without jailing him, gave him a change of clothing, and according to Livingstone, "treated me as though I were his own brother."

Proceeding west and slightly north from Cassange and crossing densely wooded country, Livingstone approached the coast on May 15 and on May 31 reached Loanda. As he had not fared well under attacks of malaria, he was urged by the English naval officers he met to return at once to England. He declined, however, noting: "My task is only half completed; I want to go back to Linyanti and try from there to press on to the east coast. Perhaps it is there that the better way is to be found for trade contacts with the interior."

For a long time Livingstone had been aware that the upper course of the Zambezi was for the most part unnavigable and frequently impassable. But he felt fairly certain that eastward from the Makololo territory, where he had first seen the river, the Zambezi might be a useful avenue of trade extending to the Indian Ocean. Though he had accomplished a tremendous feat by reaching Loanda overland, he could not end his expedition there. He had promised his Makololo porters that he would bring them back home again, even though doing so would mean traveling another two thousand miles, mostly on foot. There was never any question in Livingstone's mind that he would keep that promise, and he did.

It took them a whole year to get back to Linyanti, which was roughly a hundred miles west of the present city of Livingstone in Northern Rhodesia. No journey quite like it had ever been attempted before, and when one considers the lavish expeditions mounted by Burton and Speke it seems inconceivable that Livingstone would begin this great undertaking with only three guns and a meager amount of supplies. His secret was that he did not merely lead his men; he traveled with them. Though he could exercise authority with a hard hand when he had to, generally he treated his men as friends as well as employees. They were fellow travelers in every way.

In November, 1855, after several months' rest in Linyanti, Livingstone headed east to complete his crossing of the continent. He reached the coast at Quelimane in Mozambique six months later. His health was broken when he finally returned to England, but he was acclaimed a hero. Probably no man of his time had so fired the public imagination. He was persuaded to write an account of his experiences, and when this was published in 1857, under the title *Missionary Travels*, it was an immediate success.

Dr. Livingstone returned to the Zambezi in 1859 at the head of an expedition that included his younger brother Charles and Dr. John Kirk, who later became acting British consul at Zanzibar. Livingstone had been entrusted with the responsibility of gathering more information about the natives, exploring the possibilities for British trade in central and eastern Africa, and continuing to combat slavery.

He and his party had a steam launch called the *Ma-Robert* which they wanted to take up the Zambezi River from the African east coast. But the stiff current was too much for the vessel and she was soon forced to turn back. Now it was obvious to Livingstone that the Zambezi was wholly useless as an avenue of trade. He requested a new steamship from England, and when it arrived he sailed up the Shire River, which connects with the lower Zambezi. Then through a deep gorge in the mountains he sighted Lake Nyasa. Two years later he returned to explore his discovery.

At the beginning of 1862 he sailed east to the mouth of the Zambezi to meet his wife, who had come back from England. But by the time he reached the coast, Mary

Livingstone had caught a tropical fever, and she soon died.

Three years later, Livingstone accepted the invitation of the Royal Geographical Society to return to Central Africa—this time to clarify, once and for all, the mysteries shrouding its water courses. At fifty-three he may have seemed too old for the strenuous life of an African explorer. However, his was a hardy nature, and after the loss of his wife he had little reason to remain in England.

Much exploration had already taken place at this time in the area on either side of the chain of lakes extending from Lake Albert in the north to Lake Nyasa in the south. Baker had probed into this region from the north; Burton, Speke, and Grant had made inroads from the east; and Livingstone himself had made discoveries in the south. But a large portion of the territory was still unexplored, and Livingstone hoped now to be the man to explore it.

He had become convinced that the true source of the White Nile was actually a river that arose in Lake Mweru, southwest of Lake Tanganyika. And he knew that this river flowed into a much larger stream to the north called the Lualaba. But he knew nothing about the Lualaba except that it too flowed north. Was it the Nile or some unknown river? Could it be the Congo? (Its source had not yet been found.) That too was a possibility.

Heavy rainfall punished the countryside as Livingstone and his party cut their way toward the southern end of Lake Tanganyika. His recurring bouts with illness loosened his teeth and also slowed his advance. Soon his supplies were nearly spent, and he was forced to head for Ujiji on the eastern shore of the lake, where goods from the coast were supposedly waiting for him. In February, 1869, he reached the lake, almost toothless and nearly dead from exhaustion. He was, he wrote, "a ruckle of bones."

At Ujiji he found that his supplies had been looted. He remained there, however, in a native hut, trying to restore what he could of his health. After six months he was back on his feet. He crossed Lake Tanganyika and headed west toward the Lualaba, which he reached in March, 1871, at the town of Nyangwe.

Livingstone was hopeful, if not absolutely certain, that the Lualaba was really the upper White Nile. He was wrong, but he never knew it. From the map on page 20, it can be seen that the Lualaba is actually the upper Congo, the last of Africa's four great waterways to be explored to its source.

The weary explorer stood on the bank of the majestic

RHODES-LIVINGSTONE MUSEUM, NORTHERN RHODESIA

A brush fire blazes angrily along the bank as native boatmen pole one of Livingstone's smaller craft through the Zambezi's shallows.

river as it flowed north toward cataracts that were later named Stanley Falls. What lay beyond the mountains, beyond the thick, dark forests through which the river was known to pass? Livingstone knew he would have to attempt to find out. He tried to acquire boats for a down-river expedition, but the Arabs, suspicious that he might eventually bring other Englishmen to tap their copper mines, denied him assistance. Nor were the Negroes very helpful, so frightened were they of the arrogant slave merchants. After several fruitless weeks, Livingstone's lack of supplies forced him to abandon his plans. He returned, sick and starving, to Ujiji.

Seven hundred miles lay between him and the coast, and he was too weak to attempt the journey. He was not lost, merely unable to continue. He had to depend on the generosity of the Arabs to stay alive; he was practically reduced to begging. Then one day, less than a month after he had arrived, a spendidly equipped caravan rumbled into the lakeside village, flying, of all things, an American flag.

It was November 10, 1871. There was excitement in the

TEXT CONTINUED ON PAGE 130

How I Found Livingstone, STANLEY, 1872

Before his celebrated meeting with Stanley at Ujiji (pictured above), Dr. Livingstone found breath-taking Victoria Falls (left) on the Zambezi.

Not all the men who came to Africa were met with hostility. Some were greeted royally in the regions they visited. Giuli

Costume Antico e Moderno, FERRARIO, 1815

[F]errario painted this watercolor to show the pageantry accorded British soldiers arriving in a West African native kingdom.

TEXT CONTINUED FROM PAGE 127
village that day because the caravan was turned out so impressively. Roused by one of his servants, the old doctor went out to greet the newcomers. He stood among a group of Arabs observing the enormous train of supplies being unloaded. Suddenly a white man approached him—a short man, and stocky, with a look of supreme exultation on his face.

"Dr. Livingstone, I presume?" the white man asked.

"Yes," replied the missionary, lifting his cap slightly.

"I thank God, Doctor, I have been permitted to see you," said the white man, who identified himself as Henry Morton Stanley.

And Livingstone replied, "I feel thankful that I am here to welcome you."

This then became the most celebrated encounter in the history of African exploration. The two men were more than a generation apart, and perhaps a world apart in their thinking. Only a trick of fate had brought them together here in the heart of the African wilderness. Surely no two men could have been so different, not even Burton and Speke.

The man who called himself Henry M. Stanley was born in Wales in 1841, the year that Livingstone first went to Africa. He received what little education he had in a workhouse, where he and the other able-bodied poor exchanged their labors for food and lodging. When he was sixteen he took a job as cabin boy on a ship and went to America. There he was befriended by a rich New Orleans merchant who became his protector.

The boy, whose real name was John Rowlands, became deeply attached to the merchant—so much so that when the older man died, the boy took his name: Henry Morton Stanley.

During the next decade, Stanley's life in America was a turbulent one. He fought with both the Union and Confederate armies in the Civil War and served for a while in the U.S. Navy. He became a reporter, first in Missouri and then in New York City. As a foreign correspondent for the *New York Herald* he was soon recognized as a leading journalist.

In 1869 his editor, James Gordon Bennett Jr., sent him to Africa to cover the opening of the Suez Canal. After this he traveled east as far as India, filing stories as he went, and then returned to Africa to search for David Livingstone. The aging missionary had been heard from only twice in the four years since he had left England, and

Bennett was certain that Livingstone's rescue would provide the basis for a dramatic story.

Stanley arrived in Zanzibar in January, 1871, full of youthful optimism, and set about organizing his expedition, equipping it extravagantly. He purchased six tons of supplies, including 29,000 yards of assorted cloth, 350 pounds of copper wire, and a huge assortment of beads to trade with the natives. He also acquired a number of articles hitherto not considered essential to African exploration such as a bear skin, a Persian carpet, a bathtub, silverware, kettles for cooking, and a bottle of rare champagne to drink with Livingstone when they met.

Stanley told no one at Zanzibar that he had come to find Livingstone. The truth, and Stanley was not eager to publicize it, was that he had been sent to get a story—and get it any way he could. Bennett had told Stanley, "If he is dead, bring back every possible proof of his death." Those were Stanley's instructions when he sailed for Africa.

Americans abroad were looked on condescendingly at that time. And since Stanley had rid himself of his Welsh

Two members of Livingstone's party are poled through rapids above Victoria Falls. Dr. John Kirk (left) was the expedition's physician and botanist; Baines was its artist.

NATIONAL ARCHIVES OF RHODESIA AND NYASALAND

Harper's Weekly, 1872

This picture from a Harper's Weekly *of 1872 shows Stanley and Livingstone on the Ruzizi. The two men discovered that this river flows into Lake Tanganyika, not out of it, as Burton had believed.*

accent, he was assumed to be an American heading an American expedition. Because he seemed American, none of the Europeans in Zanzibar really thought he would survive his journey into the African interior. But this cocky little man with the barrel chest and hypnotic gray eyes was extremely gifted. Within the next six years he was to take a place beside Mungo Park and Livingstone himself in the annals of African exploration.

Stanley's first expedition followed the old trail of Burton and Speke. Aside from the help he brought Livingstone—which was considerable—this journey was important mainly because it made him world-famous and helped turn an intrepid newspaperman into a thoroughly tested explorer. Because of his initial inexperience, the fact that he got through at all was remarkable. His success was great compared with the even greater possibility of failure.

It took him nine months to reach Ujiji, during which time he frequently displayed a physical and moral courage that was worthy of any of his predecessors. However, as he confessed in his book, *How I Found Livingstone*, when he at last approached the old man on the flank of a hill overlooking Lake Tanganyika, he was terrified. He knew of Livingstone's Scottish reserve and of the old explorer's undoubted contempt for publicity, so he approached with caution and with fear. As he said, he wanted to rush forward and throw his arms about the doctor, but he was afraid of being rebuffed. So he exercised some reserve of his own, and because of this made the moment of their meeting immortal.

After he and Livingstone had exchanged greetings, Stanley ordered the bottle of champagne served. As he handed Livingstone a silver goblet, he said, "Doctor Livingstone, to your very good health, sir." Still rather dazed, the old man raised his drink and replied, "And yours."

The two men stayed in Ujiji for a few weeks while Livingstone rested and gained back some of his strength on the food Stanley had brought him. Finally the old man decided to accompany Stanley to Tabora. He agreed to wait there while Stanley journeyed to the coast, outfitted another expedition, and sent it back so Livingstone could resume his exploration into the interior.

Stanley and Livingstone reached Tabora after a two-month journey, and on March 14, 1872, they said goodbye. Stanley had to force back tears as he turned and marched away. He had spent four months and four days with the doctor. During this time, as he reported in his diary, he had been "indescribably happy." And during this time, as he was to realize later, his fascination for Africa had grown immensely. The mystery of her lakes and rivers had begun to absorb him. He would remain thus absorbed for the rest of his life.

In August, 1872, the porters and provisions that Stanley had sent from the coast reached Tabora. Now Livingstone, patiently awaiting them, could lead a new expedition southwest into Northern Rhodesia. Here he hoped to find a feeder stream that would flow toward the Lualaba. And he hoped in earnest that the Lualaba would flow eventually into Lake Albert. For if it did, then the river might well contain the secret of the White Nile's origin. However, he could not help being afraid that the Lualaba might feed into the Congo River, not the Nile. His health was failing. He had every reason to turn back—except that he had his heart set on establishing the true source of the Nile.

By April 29, 1873, Livingstone had grown so weak he had to be carried. It must have been clear to him by now that he would never finish the last task of his life. But when he died the next night—on his knees in prayer, by his bed—he had given Stanley the key to solving the last riddle of Central Africa: the course of the Lualaba-Congo River.

IX

Costume Antico e Moderno, FERRARIO, 1815

STANLEY'S WAY

When Stanley came back from Africa he was one of the most talked-of men in the Western world. Queen Victoria gave him a jeweled snuffbox, and America gave banquets in his honor and tendered him wild acclaim. There was even a play about him called *King Carrot*, which was presented in New York. But accompanying the cheers was a distinct undertone of derision—just loud enough to mar Stanley's triumph.

It was widely thought that Stanley had gone to Africa merely to make a name for himself. He had not been motivated by any particular desire to fight the slave traders or explore the wilderness. He had been sent to get a story; thus he was often regarded as an exploiter, not an explorer. And people were saying that if he could be a hero, anyone could be. Some even said that he had not really discovered Livingstone but that Livingstone had discovered him.

It was the faint sound of laughter, rather than the huzzas, that rang in Stanley's ears when he returned to Africa late in 1873. This time he was assigned to cover Britain's wars against the Ashanti tribes in the west—in present-day Ghana. The following April, on his way back to Europe, Stanley learned that Livingstone was dead and that what remained of his body was being taken to England for burial in Westminster Abbey. Stanley hastened to London to act as one of the pallbearers.

At this point a thought struck him. If he were to return to Central Africa on his own to finish Livingstone's work, no one would dare to laugh at him again. Peevishly he wrote: "What I have already endured in that accursed Africa amounts to nothing in men's estimation. Surely if I can resolve any of the problems which such travelers as Dr. Livingstone, Captains Burton, Speke, and Grant, and Sir Samuel Baker left unsettled, people must needs believe that I discovered Livingstone."

Stanley received financial support from the *New York*

Ferrario painted this European outpost near the mouth of the Congo in 1815, long before Stanley traced the river's course through the wild interior.

BOTH: *Illustrated London News*

Stanley received more than a thousand letters from men who wanted to join his next African expedition. He chose the rugged Pocock brothers, Edward (top) and Frank.

Herald and the London *Daily Telegraph*, but this time he was traveling primarily as an explorer rather than a journalist. And in this venture he proposed to accomplish twice what anyone before him had done.

First he would follow Speke and Grant's route to Lake Victoria to ascertain that this big lake was just one body of water and that the stream flowing from it at Ripon Falls was its only outlet. Then he would go south to make a final test of Burton's theory that Lake Tanganyika contained the elusive source of the Nile. After mapping the entire coast of the lake, he planned to strike west to take up Livingstone's uncompleted work on the Lualaba River. He hoped to follow the Lualaba to either the Mediterranean or the South Atlantic, depending on whether this river flowed into the Congo or the Nile.

Stanley was determined to settle the remaining doubts about the sources of the Nile and to record the entire pattern of lakes and rivers in Central Africa. For his staff he recruited two brothers, Edward and Frank Pocock, "young English boatmen of good character," and a young clerk named Frederick Barker. In September, 1874, he reached Zanzibar and began preparing the expedition. For lake and river travel he planned to use a forty-foot steel boat, the *Lady Alice*, which had been built in sections so that it could be carried overland when necessary.

Many of the men of Stanley's African staff had accompanied him on his previous expedition. When they learned the route he was now planning to follow, they were understandably anxious. The trip might take as long as ten years, they said. But Stanley assured them it would take far less time than that. And, as it turned out, he was right.

Stanley assembled eight tons of material for the expedition and hired more than 350 men to haul and guard it. They left Zanzibar for the mainland on November 12, 1874. Stanley was better equipped than he had been the first time. However, as he knew, this did not necessarily guarantee success. Within two months Edward Pocock died, and he was followed a short while later by Frederick Barker. Disease and desertion took an enormous toll of Africans, until at last only half of the original number was left—along with Frank Pocock and Stanley, who pushed gamely onward.

Arriving at Lake Victoria in March, 1875, Stanley set out by boat with some of his men. Within fifty-seven days the explorer had sailed a thousand miles all around the lake. He had proved that Lake Victoria was a single body

Illustrated London News

The Illustrated London News *published an engraving of Stanley in 1872 to commemorate the meeting with Livingstone. At that time the public wanted to know if Stanley was an ambitious journalist or a great explorer.*

of water with but two rivers flowing into and out of it: the outlet was the Victoria Nile; the inlet was the Kagera River, which entered from the west.

Stanley's discoveries at last confirmed the importance of Speke's explorations. Stanley wrote that he felt compelled to "give [Speke] credit for having understood the geography of the countries we traveled through better than any of those who so persistently opposed his hypothesis."

From Lake Victoria the expedition moved south to Lake Tanganyika, which Stanley proceeded to explore thoroughly. When he had finished, he was absolutely certain that Livingstone had been right and that there was no important river flowing out of it, nothing that could possibly be suspected as the source of the Nile. Against this evidence, Burton's theories finally collapsed, and Speke's concept of the geography of Central Africa was completely substantiated.

Now Stanley shipped the men of his party across the lake and led them toward the Lualaba River. He was close to unlocking one of nature's last secrets in Africa, for he was to follow the mysterious Lualaba and find out at last where it led.

In October, 1876, the expedition arrived at the confluence of the Luama River and the giant Lualaba. Heading downstream to Kasongo, some miles above Nyangwe, Stanley met the notorious slave trader Tippu Tib. This

Illustrated London News

As a journalist Stanley used his imagination and powers of observation to cover the wars of the British against Ashanti tribesmen like the colorful dancer at left. As an explorer Stanley used his planning abilities to manage such details as the design of the Lady Alice *(right), a forty-foot portable boat.*

PHOTO BY BILL HOMA

The muscular natives in this photograph of dugout canoes on the Congo near Stanleyville are descendants of the tribesmen who attacked Stanley in 1877.

man was said to have taken his name from the sound of spraying bullets. He was half African and half Arab, and was then one of the most feared men in all East Africa. Sixteen years later, in fact, he was close to becoming master of the entire Congo but was finally defeated by the forces of Leopold II, king of the Belgians. If Tippu Tib had known that Stanley would one day be responsible for bringing Belgians, as well as other European colonists, into the Congo, their meeting might not have been so cordial.

Stanley was eager to know what obstacles there were to a journey downstream. He suspected, of course, that the greatest obstacle might be Tippu Tib himself. Although the Arabs had not yet penetrated deeply in the Congo, they considered it their zone of influence, and they were not especially pleased to see a foreigner there. There had been others besides Livingstone who had stopped at Nyangwe, never continuing down the Lualaba. The question in Stanley's mind was why.

Tippu Tib gave the excuse that he had not wanted to see Dr. Livingstone's health endangered. This was something of an understatement, for as Stanley was soon to learn, most of the people who lived downriver were cannibals.

But Stanley was determined to go there. The slave trader argued that he lacked the manpower for such a journey, and also that he did not want to take the risk. Stanley silenced these objections by offering five thousand dollars if Tippu Tib would take him sixty marches in any direction. Tippu Tib, guided by his strong instinct for making money, finally agreed.

That night Stanley called Frank Pocock into his hut for pipes and coffee. "Now Frank, my son, sit down," said Stanley. "I am about to have a long and serious chat with you. Life and death—yours as well as mine—hang on the decision I make tonight." The choice was this: should they go north, daring the Lualaba, and hopefully gain glory, or should they go south to the safety of Katanga and give up this extremely perilous phase of their quest?

They tossed a coin, an Indian rupee: heads for the river, tails for Katanga. Six times in a row the coin turned up tails. Disappointed and unsatisfied, the men drew straws: long for north, short for south. Each time they drew only short ones. At last Stanley said, "It's no use, Frank. We'll face our destiny despite the rupees and the straws. With your help, my dear fellow, I will follow the river." So they threw away the straws, and with them Frank Pocock's last chance of ever getting home to England.

On November 5, 1876, they left Nyangwe and headed north overland to bypass the rapids that blocked them from the lower reaches of the river. Suddenly they found themselves in a thick forest that was sometimes so dark that Stanley could not see to make notes. And when they occasionally came out on a hill they could see nothing but forest around them. Tippu Tib began to grumble, for they were also being harassed by pythons, green vipers, puff adders, and howling baboons.

At last, in December, when they had gone about two hundred miles beyond Nyangwe, the slaver announced he was quitting. He had not yet fulfilled his contract but he demanded to be paid, and there was nothing much Stanley could do about it. He knew if he refused, Tippu Tib was in a position to lure most of his men away.

Stanley's trip down the Lualaba, past the seven cataracts that end at the present town of Stanleyville, was an unrelieved horror. For many months he had no idea where the river might take him. But though fearful and apprehensive, he could not turn back. He had to complete what he had begun.

Stanley and his men set out on the river on December 26, and for the next month they were plagued by the assaults of native tribesmen who wanted to eat them. The first time the party was attacked, the explorer withheld his fire. But at last he found it necessary to clear the river of the native canoes that surrounded the *Lady Alice* and the smaller boats the party also used. During the first days of the new year the men fought no less than five encounters with the cannibals.

Heroes of the Dark Continent, BUELL, 1890

Tippu Tib is shown above wearing an Arab turban and a benign smile.

One battle lasted for three hours, and though no one in the party lost his life, the prospect of having to endure similarly terrifying encounters in the months ahead was most discouraging. So was the necessity of overcoming the physical obstacles that lay ahead, the seven mighty cataracts.

When the expedition reached the first of these, the boats were hauled two miles overland on a path that the men cut through the forest and scrub. By January 8, the waters of the river were calm again, and the party returned to its boats. But by evening the second cataract lay dead ahead, and more hostile natives were gathering in force.

During the next four crucial days Stanley displayed his deep faith in himself and the amazing stubbornness for which he had already become known. He repelled the natives and drove them from their villages. Then he or-

Heroes of the Dark Continent, BUELL, 1890

Slavery was put out of business in Africa only with difficulty. Tippu Tib was one of the most powerful and long-lasting slavers, surviving until 1891. His cruelly efficient system of using Negroes to capture the slaves and lead them in chains to transshipment centers near the coast (above) differed only in detail from age-old practices in Africa. Below is an early engraving of a slave hunter leading his victim by means of a heavy wooden yoke.

BIBLIOTHEQUE NATIONALE

ganized pioneer battalions that worked night and day to cut a three-mile path through dense forest and circumvent the cataract. While the men worked, Stanley's weary rear guard fought off great hordes of attacking cannibals.

By January 20, the men had cut their way around the sixth cataract. They were now almost exactly on the equator, and they felt confident they would have smooth sailing ahead. But four days later they heard the booming of another stretch of rapids—the seventh cataract—and the whole company was in despair. Now Stanley paused to take an altitude reading. By testing the boiling point of water he was able to discern that they were 1,511 feet above sea level. This was about fourteen feet below the known level of the Nile at Gondokoro, much farther north. Now

As the Congo spills into a cataract called Foulakary Falls (below), it becomes a roaring torrent. It is but one of the many cataracts that Stanley met on his way to the sea.

This "bird-head" throwing knife is a weapon used by Congo tribesmen.

THE MUSEUM OF PRIMITIVE ART, NEW YORK

FRENCH EMBASSY PRESS AND INFORMATION SERVICE

there was little doubt. Stanley and his party were on the Congo, not the Nile. This was dispiriting. If they had been on the Nile, some sort of aid could have been expected to reach them in a matter of weeks. On the Congo, they knew they had many more months of travel ahead, and perhaps hundreds of rapids to overcome.

By January 28, Stanley had skirted the last major obstacle, the seventh cataract. Although he did not know it, his way was clear now for a thousand miles. There would be no more geographical obstacles until the party reached another series of rapids on the lower part of the river, near the present city of Leopoldville. But there were obstacles, nonetheless: more angry tribesmen eager to do battle with the strange and frightening white men.

During one hundred-mile stretch Stanley and his men fought eight pitched battles. Their stock of ammunition was almost depleted and they were running out of weapons, but actually their most potent weapon was Stanley himself. He held his party together by the sheer force of his personality. And like Livingstone, he was not above threatening to fire on his men if they became frightened enough to scatter and flee.

The men stayed with him, but the continual combat wearied and embittered them. Sometimes they had only a few hours' peace a day. At one point Stanley wrote in his journal, "Livingstone called floating down the Lualaba a foolhardy feat. So it has proved indeed, and I pen these lines with half a feeling that they will never be read by any man . . . Day and night we are stunned with the dreadful drumming which announces our arrival and presence on their waters. Either bank is equally powerful. To go from the right bank to the left bank is like jumping from the frying pan into the fire . . ."

Fortunately the situation did not last long, and soon the tribes they met along the river were more subdued—or at least less aggressive and hostile. One day they asked a friendly native chief what this river was called, and he replied, "*Ikutu ya Kongo*." Stanley had compiled a glossary of words of the local language, but he did not need to be a linguist to know what the chief was saying. Nor was he very much surprised.

By March the party was only about six degrees longitude from the known mouth of the Congo River—about 450 air miles—quite close to it considering the great distance the men had already covered. But they were still more than a thousand feet above sea level. Obviously there were treacherous falls and rapids ahead of them before they could reach the sea. There would be no more bouts with native tribes; now their bitterest enemy would be the river itself.

At this point it was important that they devise some means of holding back their boats from the rushing waters. They learned eventually to use rattan hawsers to leash each boat; the men walked along the shore holding tight to the leashes, and the boats were saved from the river's fury. This system worked well on the shorter stretches of rough water, but frequently the boats had to be pulled out and carried overland.

Despite the precautions taken by the men, their supplies were dwindling—more by loss than consumption—and they could not help losing a boat now and then. At one particularly violent section of river, a seventy-five-foot canoe was jerked from the fifty pairs of hands that leashed it, and it swept away. And on April 12 the sturdy *Lady Alice*, containing most of the supplies, and Stanley himself, was torn loose from its cables and whirled several miles through the turbulent river. When the ship was finally shunted into calm waters, Stanley was rescued. For hours his men had feared he was dead. He was a hard-driving disciplinarian, but after serving him for nearly three years, they had developed a genuine fondness for him.

Some days later the group came to a great rapids that plunged through a deep chasm. It would have been impossible to follow the river at this point, but an overland route did not appear to be a satisfactory alternative. The banks on either side of the river rose steeply and seemed impassable. But Stanley managed to coerce some nearby tribes to help him and his men, and together they moved the entire caravan over one of the tall embankments at a rate of five hundred to eight hundred yards a day.

In the meantime Frank Pocock had begun to suffer from ulcers on his feet. At one set of rapids Stanley left him behind to be carried overland in a hammock. This seemed shameful to Pocock, so after Stanley had gone ahead, he insisted on traveling the dangerous stretch in a boat. The boat capsized, and Frank Pocock drowned. His body was recovered some days later, and Stanley was grief-stricken.

The young man's death was a blow to everyone, in fact. With Frank gone the men simply lost spirit. They felt sure they were going to die anyway, so why should they continue draining their energy in such a futile endeavor? When Stanley's boat broke loose again and was spun downstream

Stanley drew this sketch of an incident on his horror-filled Congo journey: fifty-two native canoes (background) filled with chanting cannibals attacked his expedition.

in the rapids, the men were certain he was doomed. And by this time they were so exhausted that they hardly cared. They would follow him to oblivion soon enough, they thought. But suddenly Stanley was spotted walking back along the shore, looking as cocky as ever; they could not help being heartened. Perhaps they would make it after all if they stayed with him. So onward they went, following their leader.

By the end of July the boats had to be abandoned, and the men were traveling overland again. Now they were desperate for food, and they had almost nothing of value left to buy it with. And what was worse, they knew they would get very little for their trading goods because here, near the Portuguese settlement on the coast, only rum and modern weapons were considered valuable merchandise.

A few days later they became so weak from hunger they could not go on, though help lay but a few miles ahead. Stanley finally persuaded a chieftain to carry a letter forward to Boma, or Embomma, and wrote this message by the light of a lamp made of rotted sheeting dipped in palm butter:

Village of Nsanda, August 4, 1877

To any Gentleman who speaks English at Embomma

Dear Sir,

I have arrived at this place from Zanzibar with 115 souls . . . We are now in a state of imminent starvation. We can buy nothing from the natives, for they laugh at our kinds of cloth, beads, and wire. . . . I am told there is an Englishman at Embomma, and as you are a Christian and a gentleman, I beg you not to disregard my request . . . [I want] fifteen man-loads of rice or grain to fill their pinched bellies immediately . . . The supplies must arrive within two days, or I may have a fearful time of it among the dying . . .

Yours sincerely,
H. M. Stanley,
Commanding Anglo-American
Expedition for Exploration
of Africa

P.S. You may not know my name; therefore I add, I am the person that discovered Livingstone in 1871. H.M.S.

Help came from Boma a few days after Stanley's letter was sent, and on August 12, 1877, the entire party reached the Atlantic. They had been traveling 999 days, nearly three years. But their journey was not over. Stanley had made a pledge that if he survived the expedition he would return his men to Zanzibar. He acquired a ship and sailed around the Cape of Good Hope into the Indian Ocean. He deposited the survivors of his expedition at Zanzibar, as he had promised, and then proceeded to England.

Stanley was to return to Africa several times more, but this expedition marked the peak of his career as an explorer. For in a single river-journey he had succeeded in solving what remained of the mystery of Africa's waterways. Now there could be no doubt: the Lualaba, which rose in Northern Rhodesia, joined the Congo and flowed across Africa to the South Atlantic; and the White Nile rose in Lake Victoria, was joined by waters of the Blue Nile, and meandered north through the Sudan and Egypt to the Mediterranean.

The continent's four great rivers—the Zambezi, the

Baines often painted Livingstone's great discovery, Victoria Falls. Here the artist shows natives hunting buffalo on the chasm's brink.

Niger, the Nile, and the Congo—had now been explored, their courses traced entirely. There were still blank spaces on the map, but much fewer than before, and no great geographic puzzles remained to be solved. Exploration continued far into the twentieth century—in the mountains and deserts and into the dark, forbidding jungles. But it can be said that when Henry Morton Stanley returned to Zanzibar on November 26, 1877, three years after he had left it, the great age of African discovery was completed.

NATIONAL ARCHIVES OF RHODESIA AND NYASALAND

Dixon Denham pursues a tall, spotted creature he called a cameleopard.

ACKNOWLEDGMENTS

The Editors are deeply grateful to the curators and staff members of the many private and public collections in which paintings, sculpture, and rare exploration journals of value to this book were found. Special thanks are owed to the following individuals and organizations for their assistance:

Royal Geographical Society
William Fehr, Fehr Collection, Cape Town
South London Art Gallery, Camberwell Borough Council
E. Cole, New York Public Library, Rare Book Division
Seymour Kurtz, The Museum of Primitive Art, New York
E. Burke, National Archives of Rhodesia and Nyasaland
R. A. Skelton, Keeper of the Map Division, British Museum
Mrs. Daphne Strutt, Durban Old House Museum
Dr. Gordon Gibson, Paul Oesher, Smithsonian Institution
Gervas Clay, Rhodes-Livingstone Museum, Northern Rhodesia
Boies Penrose, Devon, Pennsylvania
Katie Jarratt, Department of Information, Republic of South Africa
Gertrude Rosenthal, The Baltimore Museum of Art
Dorothy Miner, The Walters Art Gallery, Baltimore
Colin Turnbull, The American Museum of Natural History
Drs. Fernando Batalha, Virgilio Canna Martins, Luanda, Angola
Dr. John Walker, National Gallery of Art
E. Bongard, Pennsylvania Historical Society
French Embassy Press and Information Service

Special research and photography: New York—Geoffrey Clements; London—Maureen Green, Zoltan Wegner

Maps by Herbert Borst

FURTHER REFERENCE

Readers interested in further exploring African primitive art or in viewing exhibitions relating to African history will find collections in many American cities. Among the fine museums of African art are The Museum of Primitive Art, N.Y.; the Cincinnati Art Museum; the Denver Art Museum; the Santa Barbara Museum of Art; the University of Pennsylvania, University Museum, Philadelphia; The Baltimore Museum of Art; Harvard University, Peabody Museum of Archaeology and Ethnology, Cambridge, Mass.; the Chanute African Museum, Chanute, Kan.; the Brooklyn Museum; and the Albion College Art Museum, Albion, Mich. African natural history exhibits can be seen at The American Museum of Natural History, N.Y.; the Fort Worth Children's Museum; the Children's Nature Museum of York County, Rock Hill, S.C.; the Snow Museum, Oakland, Calif.; the Milwaukee Public Museum; and Zoorama Inc., New Market, Va. Collections dealing more particularly with exploration can be found at the Smithsonian Institution; the Peabody Museum's East India Marine Hall, Salem, Mass.; and the New York Public Library, Rare Book Division.

For those who wish to read more about the exploration of Africa, the following books are recommended:

Axelson, Eric. *South African Explorers*. Oxford University Press, 1954.

Baker, Samuel. *The Albert N'Yanza*. Horizon, 1962.

Baulin, Jacques. *The Arab Role in Africa*. Penguin, 1962.

Briggs, Lloyd Cabot. *Tribes of the Sahara*. Harvard University Press, 1960.

Burton, Richard. *Personal Narrative of a Pilgrimage to Al-Madinah and Meccah*. Edited by Isabel Burton. Dover, 1962.

Debenham, Frank. *Discovery and Exploration*. Doubleday, 1960.

Dinesen, Isak. *Out of Africa*. Modern Library, 1952; *Shadows on the Grass*. Random, 1961.

Gunther, John and others. *Meet North Africa*. Harper, 1957.

Kane, Robert S. *Africa from A to Z*. Doubleday, 1961.

Kimble, George H. T. *Tropical Africa*. (2 volumes). Twentieth-Century, 1960.

Leuzinger, Elsy. *The Art of Africa*. Crown, 1960.

Mannix, D. P. and Cowley, M. *Black Cargoes*. Viking, 1962.

Miller, R., editor. *The Travels of Mungo Park*. Dutton, 1960.

Moorehead, Alan. *The Blue Nile*. Harper, 1962; *The White Nile*. Harper, 1960.

Paton, Alan. *Land and People of South Africa*. Lippincott, 1955.

Perham, M. and Simmons, J. *African Discovery*. Faber and Faber, 1957.

Richards, C. G. and Place, J. *East African Explorers*. Oxford University Press, 1960.

Schiffers, Dr. Heinrich. *The Quest for Africa*. Odhams Press Ltd.

Stanley, Richard and Neame, A., editors. *The Newly Discovered Exploration Diaries of H. M. Stanley*. Vanguard, 1962.

Sterling, Thomas. *Stanley's Way*. Atheneum, 1960.

Sykes, Sir Percy. *A History of Exploration*. Routledge & Kegan Paul, Ltd., 1949.

Syme, Ronald. *African Traveler*. Morrow, 1962.

INDEX

Bold face indicates pages on which maps or illustrations appear